Microcomputer
Assembly Language
Programming

Microcomputer Assembly Language Programming

Gary Elfring

President
Elfring Consulting, Inc.
St. Charles, Illinois

VNR VAN NOSTRAND REINHOLD COMPANY

Copyright © 1984 by Van Nostrand Reinhold Company Inc.

Library of Congress Catalog Card Number: 84-3532
ISBN: 0-442-22261-0

Manufactured in the United States of America

Published by Van Nostrand Reinhold Company Inc.
135 West 50th Street
New York, New York 10020

Van Nostrand Reinhold Company Limited
Molly Millars Lane
Wokingham, Berkshire RG11 2PY, England

Van Nostrand Reinhold
480 Latrobe Street
Melbourne, Victoria 3000, Australia

Macmillan of Canada
Division of Gage Publishing Limited
164 Commander Boulevard
Agincourt, Ontario M1S 3C7, Canada

15 14 13 12 11 10 9 8 7 6 5 4 3 2 1

Library of Congress Cataloging in Publication Data

Elfring, Gary.
  Microcomputer assembly language programming.

  Includes index.
  1. Microcomputers – Programming. 2. Microprocessors –
Programming. 3. Assembler language (Computer program
language) I. Title.
QA76.6.E436   1984   001.64′2   84-3532
ISBN 0-442-22261-0

This book is dedicated to
my wife and son
Mary
&
Matthew
and two thirds of the three stooges of consulting
Art
Mark

Preface

In 1980 I began teaching a series of seminars in what I like to call Advanced Microprocessor Programming Techniques. These seminars were designed to teach advanced techniques for working with assembly language on microprocessors. I chose assembly language as the basis for the course for an important reason. It seems that—regardless of which languages are best suited to a particular task—many microprocessor programs are now being written in assembly language.

A great number of books on programming and microprocessors appear every year. However, the majority of these books fall into one of two categories: they are either introductory books (whether for microcomputers, BASIC, or assembly language), or technical books aimed at hardware design and engineering. There are very few books on what to do after you learn to program. Thus a book on advanced assembly-language programming seemed appropriate. Some source of information should exist to help both the beginning and the experienced programmer to improve their assembly-language programming techniques.

Programming microprocessors in assembly language is a tedious task at best. It is also fundamentally different from working with minicomputers and mainframes in assembly language. The microcomputer system is a hardware-oriented, limited-resource world. The assembly-language programmer must cope with proper program design, structured programming techniques, and most of all, hardware. The microcomputer communicates with the outside world through its hardware. Thus the assembly-language programmer will have to understand and utilize this hardware to develop his programs. The hardware on microprocessor systems is so involved with the software that it is not unusual to debug programs with the aid of an oscilloscope.

This book is a guide to better assembly-language programming on microprocessors. It is not an introduction to this topic, nor will it teach basic assembly-language programming. All the programming techniques presented here are specifically designed for the microprocessor environment. This book assumes some knowledge of assembly-language programming. While the examples in the book utilize 8080 mnemonics, it is *not* necessary to know 8080 assembly language to understand the techniques presented here. The 8080 was chosen because many people are familiar with its instruction set or those of its close relatives, the Z80, 8088, and 8086. Once you know one microprocessor assembly language, it is not difficult to switch to the others, so the examples presented here should be of use to everyone.

Microcomputer Assembly-Language Programming is designed for all persons involved in microprocessor programming. Sooner or later nearly all programmers will have to get involved with some tricky piece of hardware that requires assembly language to make it work. Hopefully, the techniques presented here will be of some use.

The book is divided into nine chapters. Chapters 1 and 2 are an introduction to microprocessor assembly-language programming concepts and a general guide to this type of programming. Chapter 3 covers top-down design for microprocessors. The fourth chapter presents an adaptation of structured programming—techniques that have been modified to work well with assembly language. Chapter 5 treats the software development process in both the hardware and software aspects. Chapters 6 and 7 deal with using assembler features and various assembly-language programming techniques. Chapter 8 is an introduction to real-time executives and using them with assembly language. Finally, the last chapter discusses using high-level languages and assembly language together; they make a great team, when used properly.

Contents

Microcomputer Assembly Language Programming

1
Introduction

WORKING WITH MICROPROCESSORS

Every year microprocessors have a greater impact on society. As they become more prevalent, they expose more people to the concept of programming. It would not be surprising to see a microcomputer in most homes within the next five years. While there will be hundreds of different types of computers, they will all have one thing in common: each system will need some type of program to make it function.

This increase in computer systems is going to involve a large number of programs. Who is going to write these programs and how will they be written? What type of programming techniques will be used to design, code, and debug these programs? Is there some generalized programming philosophy that can make some of the chores of programming easier?

In the past, programming philosophy was seen as an important topic. It was felt that very few, if any, programmers could ever afford their own computer; they would always work for an employer to make a computer perform some useful function. Programmers were expected to perform a service; their work should be of a certain minimum caliber and understandable by others. After all, it was for those other people that the program was intended. Thus overall programming philosophy was a very important part of a programmer's life. Programmers and their software had to interact with the real world in some organized manner.

Then along came the microprocessor revolution: everyone could afford their own computer system. With a computer readily available, people started writing programs for their own gratification. Slowly but surely, this seemed to erode the necessity for a generalized programming philosophy. If you write the majority of programs for yourself, why bother to conform to a restrictive set of programming

1

rules? Who will look at the program but yourself? Since you wrote it, you will always be able to understand it.

Another blow to universal programming philosophy came from the sheer number of people who became involved in programming. Since the majority of these people had no formal training in programming, they saw no need for what they considered to be nonproductive programming techniques. It takes time to properly comment and document a program. It takes even more time to do a proper program design or implement structured programming techniques. Most of these programming techniques were seen as either a waste of time to implement, or simply not applicable to the microprocessor environment.

How many of these criticisms are valid? Is an advanced programming philosophy of any use with respect to a microcomputer? A close examination of many professional programming firms will show that a large number of them use structured programming, top-down design, and other features of an advanced programming philosophy. Why are some programmers going to these techniques, then, while others ignore them? And if these techniques do not work well with microprocessors, is it possible to adapt them so that they will work?

The purpose of this book is to answer these questions on programming philosophy and to introduce the programmer to the special problems associated with microprocessor programming. This book emphasizes programming microprocessors in assembly language. Most of the techniques described here have been adapted to work specifically with assembly language. While these techniques will work just as well in most high-level languages, the examples here will deal strictly with assembly language.

Why assembly language? Microprocessors and their programs are often heavily hardware-oriented. The microcomputer has a limited set of resources, of which many of the programs being written need to make the greatest possible use. Fully utilizing all the features of a given microprocessor often involves the use of assembly language. Only assembly language can guarantee that one section of a program will run in a fixed amount of time.

A second reason for using assembly language throughout this book involves the languages in which programmers choose to write their software. Most microprocessor programmers either start out with assembly language, or at one time or another are forced to use it. Programming in assembly language, however, has a great number of disadvantages: assembly language is hard to follow, difficult to understand, and easy to make mistakes in. Since such programming is so difficult and most programmers use it at one time or another, some form of help is needed. This book will supply that help.

Finally, specialized hardware devices are frequently used in conjunction with microprocessors. Use of specialized hardware can greatly reduce the complexity and amount of software needed to perform a given function. Unfortunately, often this hardware can be utilized only through assembly language. Either a higher level language cannot keep up with the speed of this device, or the language has no provisions for initializing and utilizing hardware. Thus assembly language can become a necessary component of your software.

GOOD PROGRAMS

The Programmer

This book is designed to increase your general programming skills and specifically to aid you in assembly-language programming. This implies that by reading this book you can become a better programmer. What exactly is a good programmer? Are there certain characteristics that mark a good programmer? Is a good assembly-language programmer different from any other type of programmer? Here is a list of characteristics that might make a programmer good.

1. A good programmer is logical.
2. A good programmer knows how to solve problems.
3. A good programmer works well with others.
4. A good programmer communicates well.
5. A good programmer programs quickly.
6. A good programmer is methodical.
7. A good programmer "understands" machines.
8. A good programmer documents programs.
9. A good programmer writes good programs.
10. A good programmer is reliable.
11. A good programmer works quickly.
12. A good programmer meets schedules.

Are any or all of the items on this list a requirement for being a good programmer? It is very unlikely that all these items are required, since many good programmers lack one or more of the above characteristics. It might even be possible to be a good programmer, yet have none of the characteristics listed here. Most people will even agree that item 9 does not necessarily have to be true: A good program does not necessarily imply that the person producing it was good at his or her work.

Difficult as it may be to describe what a good programmer is, most programmers have no trouble judging the work of other programmers. Especially in the microprocessor environment, they seem quick to pass judgment on other programmers and programs. Programmers that use a few too many bytes or write slightly inefficient programs are often condemned. Does using a few extra bytes or being slightly less efficient than someone else make you a poor programmer? Perhaps the definition of a good programmer has more to do with the definition of what makes a program good than with the individual characteristics of the programmer.

The Program

What defines a good program? Is there some simple way to determine if a program is good, bad, or mediocre? If a program performs its function, do distinctions about its relative quality have any meaning? The easiest way to determine whether a *working* program is good or not is to give it to another programmer to maintain. You will quickly get an opinion on whether or not the program is good. Of course, once a problem is solved, most programmers can arrive at a better solution by examining the first one. Thus the judgment of program quality may be slightly biased.

A list of good program qualities may help resolve the definition of a good program:

1. The program works.
2. The program works well.
3. The program is debugged.
4. The program is well documented.
5. The program is understandable.

6. The program is expandable.
7. The program is easy to use.
8. The program is user-friendly.
9. The program is easy to maintain.
10. The program is efficient.

These program qualities are listed in their relative order of importance. A careful look at this list shows that these characteristics can be divided into two different categories: some items have to do with how a program was written, while others describe how the program operates. How a program was written typically has no meaning to the end user of that program. It is, however, important to the organization that created and maintains this program. On the other hand, actual program operation is not very important to a programmer, who is rarely the end user of this product or system. The programmer is more concerned with how the program was written. Both how a program was written and how it now operates are very important in determining whether the program is good or bad.

The first two items on this list seem to be saying the same thing, but there is a major distinction between a program that works and one that works well. Programs that work well are much more likely to be good programs than ones that just work. Note that a program must at least work before it can be considered good! No matter how well written it is, or what special features it may have, a program that doesn't work is not a good program.

Another feature of a good program is that it is debugged. Very few, if any, programs are ever completely debugged, but a few bugs will not keep a program from being considered good. If the bugs do not appear often and do not seriously impede program operation, then the program may be good. But a program cannot be considered good if it has serious bugs in it. Serious bugs will usually brand the product or device as unreliable or not functional. This type of program will be used less and less often until it is either totally forgotten or repaired.

A good program should be well documented. Very few programmers have perfect memories. I find it hard to remember how a program I wrote three months ago works. It is thus very possible that, as I finish a software project, I will have forgotten how parts of it function. I use documentation as an aid for myself. It is much easier to investigate, change, and debug well-documented software than it is to depend upon an imperfect memory. Another reason for documenting your programs is that you will probably not be the only one to work with this software; other programmers will work with it, too. It is easier to document the program at the time you write it than to explain it to someone at a later date.

Programs should be understandable. Not everyone is a superprogrammer or certified genius. Since other programmers will usually be involved with your program throughout its life, it pays to make the program as simple as possible. A simple program is understandable. If there are two ways to perform a given task, the simpler one should be preferred. This helps ensure that other programmers will understand your software in the future.

Another nice program feature is expandability. A program that is easy to expand is a joy to work with. Almost all programs must be maintained, which implies that new features will be added at some time. Programs that are designed to be added to greatly reduce the programmer's work load.

A program that is easy to use is often considered good. Few people take the time to read a manual before they try to operate the software: the usual attack is to plug the software in and see if you can make it work. A program that is easy to use will avoid problems arising when end users neglect to read the documentation.

Good programs should be user-friendly. The program should welcome, not insult, the user. A user-friendly program gives positive feedback. Instead of sounding a buzzer on an incorrect entry, why not offer a bit of *polite* help: inform the user that the entry was incorrect and offer a list of possible correct entries. A help or HELP command or feature can also make a program more user-friendly. A user who gets lost or confused should be able to ask the machine for help. This is what making intelligent devices is all about.

Programs that are easy to maintain are often considered good. Usually such a program is well documented and understandable. There are other aspects to a maintainable program as well. Maintenance functions can be designed into a program so as to allow all hardware inputs and outputs to be exercised. Similarly, maintenance features can be added to a program that exercise and test various pieces of the software. This can greatly help to debug new features added to the original software. The test routines can ensure that most basic program functions have not been affected by the new software features.

The final feature of a good program is efficiency. While a good program does not have to be efficient, it cannot hurt to be so. As long as program efficiency does not interfere with the other aspects of a good program, it is a desirable goal. An efficient program has more available processing time, so that more new features or program modifications can be made to it.

MICROPROCESSOR PROGRAMMING TECHNIQUES

The previous sections have given you some idea of what is involved in writing a good program. The next question you might ask is, how do I go about writing a good program for a microprocessor? Are there special programming techniques that will enable me to produce a better program? Should the programming techniques I use for micro-processors be any different from the ones I use on a minicomputer?

There is a collection of advanced programming techniques that has been used on mainframes and minicomputes for years. Some of these techniques embody simple common sense, while others are based on actual advances in software engineering. For the most part these tech-niques have been infrequently used with microprocessors, because most of them apply only to work in high-level languages. Assembly-language programming techniques are not often stressed for mini-computers and mainframes.

But these advanced programming techniques do offer a significant improvement over other methods. They can be modified to work well with microprocessors, if two different types of adaptation are made. First, they must be changed so that they apply more readily to assembly-language programming. Second, they must be modified so as to be more hardware-oriented.

This book presents a collection of advanced programming tech-niques specifically adapted to the microprocessor environment and assembly language. Wherever possible, these techniques have been modified to take advantage of the hardware orientation of micro-processors. The topics covered include the following:

1. A general guide to microprocessor programming
2. Top-down program design for microprocessors
3. Structured programming in assembly language
4. Relocatable assemblers
5. Writing and using macros
6. General assembly-language tips and techniques
7. Real-time executives
8. Mixing high-level languages with an assembler
9. Review of high-level languages

The general guide to microprocessor programming covers various techniques used to define a problem, code a program, and debug the software. Ideas for naming variables, commenting programs, and developing test procedures are presented. A short one-page summary of this guide is also included.

A modified top-down program-design technique is described in Chapter 3. This combination top-down, bottom-up design technique is presented specifically for microprocessors. Data-flow diagrams and program-module hierarchy charts are also discussed.

Structured programming techniques for assembly language are presented in Chapter 4. The various aspects of structured programming are described and adapted specifically to the microprocessor programmed in assembly language.

Software development is an important process. Chapter 5 describes the various aspects of this process, with a general coverage of both the hardware and software requirements of software development.

Chapter 6 contains information on how to make the best use of your present assembler. Relocatable assemblers are discussed along with reasons for their use. Macro definition and use are also explained. Numerous examples show how to write and use these powerful tools.

Specialized assembly-language programming techniques are presented in Chapter 7. Program organization and initialization is discussed. True and false flags are covered, along with table structures and their uses. Finally, several programming techniques are presented that take advantage of special types of microprocessor instructions.

Chapter 8 discusses real-time executives. These powerful operating systems can greatly ease programming chores on microprocessors. Executive concepts of concurrency, priority, suspension, and reentrant code are covered. Popular real-time executive features are also discussed.

Chapter 9 deals with high-level languages. Techniques for mixing assembly-language and high-level languages are presented. A general review of high-level languages is also provided. The chapter concludes with a discussion of preprocessors and their use with assembly language.

2
A Programmer's Guide

Assembly-language programming and microprocessors are a natural pair. Both microprocessors and assembly language are extremely hardware-oriented. Only assembly language gives a programmer complete control over the hardware that is part of his product or device, as well as the amount of time the program will take to execute. Since microprocessors have limited resources, this time control can be very important.

The purpose of any programming language is to help you write programs. A good programming language lets you write programs faster, more easily, and with less errors than does a poor language. A good programming language makes your life as a programmer easier. Assembly language, however, does not really meet any of these requirements. Programming in assembly language is typically a dull and tedious job. There are so many details to take care of that errors seem inevitable.

Why are so many programs written in assembly language? There are several reasons, not all of which are valid. The problems associated with hardware control are frequently mentioned as one reason for using assembly language. Another reason is the need for some type of real-time control in a program. Often the programmer is familiar only with assembly language, or the high-level languages he does know are not available for his particular microprocessor. Finally, some people are comfortable with only one language, and for microprocessor programming that one language is, more often than not, assembly language.

Programming in assembly language is not an easy task. Any techniques or rules that aid in assembly-language programming should be of great value to the programmer. This chapter contains a list of programming techniques and rules that are easy to learn and apply. Most programmers practice some of these techniques every day. By using all these techniques, you can reduce both the problems and the tedium associated with assembly-language programming.

The following list of techniques is broken down into three sections that cover approaching a problem, coding a program, and debugging a program. The order of the items is not necessarily that of relative importance. Certain techniques or rules may be more important in one program than another. One important thing to remember is: don't break the rules before you have learned them.

Approaching the Problem
1. Define the problem first.
2. Separate programming from problem solving.
3. Use a structured approach.
4. Design for the end user.
5. Use programming teams for system design.
6. Separate the logical from the physical.
7. Consider a hardware approach.

Coding the Program
1. Program in modules.
2. Use header blocks.
3. Comment your program.
4. Use good mnemonic names for variables.
5. Be consistent.
6. Avoid unnecessary jumps.
7. Avoid tricks.
8. Build in debugging aids.
9. Start simply and work toward the complex.

Debugging the Program
1. Hand-check the program before running it.
2. Write down test procedures.
3. Check the program in an orderly manner.
4. Develop debugging software.

APPROACHING THE PROBLEM

Define the Problem First

The whole purpose behind writing a program is to solve some type of problem. Obviously, before you can solve a problem, you   must understand what that problem is. Before a programmer can write a program, he must understand what the product or system he is working on is suppose to do. Microprocessor-based systems are a lot more physically oriented than other types of commuter systems. Thus understanding what your product is supposed to do for a microprocessor-based system may involve learning the actual operation of the device you are building.

To understand what a system or product is supposed to do, the programmer must envision how it will operate. He must ask questions such as, what is the purpose of this device? How will this device function and how will it interact with its operator? He also needs to envision physically what the device will look like.

To get this information, the programmer will be required to ask questions about the product's operation and function. The typical specifications supplied by management, marketing, or sales personnel rarely include enough information to design a system. Usually it is up to the programmer to ask the questions needed to gather enough information to write the program.

One of the difficulties with this type of approach is that it is entirely up to the programmer to avoid any possible faults in the operation and function of the system. Unless the programmer thoroughly understands system operation, it will be difficult to avoid faults in it. He may end up with numerous logical contradictions in how it operates. While a programmer can discover and correct some of these logical contradictions, it is often difficult to find all of them, since he is not totally familiar with the proposed device.

One solution to this type of problem is to make the programmer responsible for writing out a definition of the device operation in English. Since the programmer is the one required to gather most of the information defining the problem, it is up to him to physically define the problem in English. This written definition then becomes the basis for the entire machine. The definition should be supplied to management, marketing, or sales. They should be allowed to comment on this written specification before any further work is done on the system. The whole purpose of all these steps is to get an understanding and a written definition of what the problem really is, before the programmer starts to write or design the program.

Separate Programming from Problem Solving

Keep in mind that two different things should be considered when starting out on a microprocessor-based system: programming and problem solving. They should not be confused. An obvious first step in any project is to solve the problem. Once there is a simple solution to the problem itself, programming or coding should come easily. A number of programmers, however, become impatient with this type of approach. Rather than attempting to solve the problem first, they jump into the coding and try to solve a problem with programming techniques.

Such programming is based on a poor assumption. It assumes that if you can code programs well, the problem solution or design will follow. Unfortunately, when you think about it, this is exactly the opposite of the real case. Once a problem is solved or there is a design solution to it, anyone can code a program implementing that solution. Problem solving, however, is a much more complicated task and is not usually taught in schools. It takes experience to learn to solve problems well.

Use a Structured Approach

Two different techniques can greatly simplify your assembly-language programming task: the combination top-down, bottom-up design approach, and a structured programming approach modified for use with assembly language.

The combination top-down, bottom-up design technique is a specialized design methodology developed for use with assembly-language programming on microprocessor systems. It is a modification of the top-down design technique used on minicomputers and mainframes. Because microprocessors are very often hardware-oriented, some modification of the original top-down technique is needed. Varying hardware environments can greatly affect the basic design of a system. Hardware, in fact, is often part of the overall software design on microprocessors. These techniques are described in much greater detail in Chapter 3.

Structured programming also needs to be adapted for assembly language. The structured programming techniques can greatly aid and simplify a normal assembly-language program. The use of structured programming with assembly language is discussed in much greater detail in Chapter 4.

Design for the End User

This idea often seems to get lost, as more and more programmers struggle to implement greater and greater programs. A program is a solution to a problem, and it should also be a solution for the end user. The end user is typically not a microprocessor programmer. He is not interested in advanced programming techniques. The end user wants a simple solution to his problem.

For a programmer to correctly design and implement a program, he needs to identify with the particular end user of the device. A program written for systems users of a mainframe will be designed with many more subtleties and complicated features than a microprocessor-controlled blender designed for the average household. The microprocessor programmer needs to know and understand the individual user who will end up with his product. In many cases it is the end user who will control whether or not the product has numerous special or complicated features. If the end user is not capable of using these special features, there is no use implementing them in the system.

Equally important, microprocessor programs should for the most part be usable without any manual or instruction whatsoever by a first-time user. When you sit down to write with a new assembler or a new compiler, you very rarely look at the manual. The average person using a microprocessor product does exactly the same thing. The person to whom this microprocessor-based product is sold will probably not look at the manual until he gets in trouble, by which time he may have lost patience with your program. Thus your program should be user-friendly and help guide a new user through the instructions needed to operate the device. This does *not* mean that you should not develop a good manual to explain the use and operation of the product. Even though very few people will initially read your manual, eventually they will have to resort to it to operate some of the more complex features of the machine. Therefore there should be a manual to go along with it and the manual should be easy to understand.

Use Programming Teams for System Design

A small group of two or three can typically produce a much better system design for a microprocessor-based product than any individual, because of the interplay of ideas among members of the group. A group can arrive at multiple solutions to the same problem. This then offers the choice of which is the best solution or approach to the problem. Another advantage of a group is that it is much more difficult to lock onto a single idea or single solution, or to arrive at a poor solution.

Separate the Logical from the Physical

This simple technique was developed a number of years ago on mainframe and minicomputers. It has not been used very much in microprocessor-based systems. The basic concept is quite simple: when writing a program, separate the portion of the program that makes decisions from the portion that controls hardware.

The logical side of the program has no need to understand how hardware functions. If the logical side of the program needs to make use of, say, a switch input, it should simply call a subroutine. The subroutine should return a true or false value, depending upon whether or not the switch is set. This isolates the decision-making portion of the program from the hardware.

The physical section of the program is responsible for controlling all the various hardware devices throughout the microprocessor system. Its sole function is to work with hardware. This section of the program is in total control of all software that deals with hardware. It may consist of numerous subroutines that test individual hardware devices, returning a status of true or false. This section of the program will also be responsible for initializing these hardware devices. It may also control basic functions such as interrupt-service routines and timing control.

There are two reasons for separating the logical section of the program from the physical. First, such separation simplifies your program logic. Second, it is best to isolate as much software as possible from the hardware, so the logical section can then be tested without the need of any hardware-control software. Likewise, the physical section of the program may then be tested on its own. Keeping the logical separate from the physical side of your programs reduces their complexity. Simple programs are easier to debug and maintain.

Consider a Hardware Approach

Hardware can often solve difficult software problems. This type of solution has not been typically available in minicomputers and mainframes. If you need some complicated piece of software on these computers, you do not really have the option of replacing that piece of software with hardware.

Microprocessors, however, are somewhat different. They easily interface to the numerous new hardware devices developed in recent years. Depending upon the number of units or devices of your microprocessor-based systems sold per year, additional hardware may be much cheaper than additional software.

For example, suppose your software needed to count pulses coming from some external hardware device. Rather than write an interrupt routine to count these pulses, it would probably be much easier to have the counts run into a counter timer chip. This chip can take a great deal of the software overhead away from you. Essentially the hardware device is used to simplify your software.

Another example of this type of approach can be found in a hardware multiply routine. In some microprocessor-based systems it becomes necessary to do a large number of multiplications in a fixed period of time. Rather than write a complicated multiply routine and worry about the amount of time that this routine will take to work, you can purchase a simple single-chip device which will do the work for you. Often the cost per system of this hardware device would be more than outweighed by the cost per unit of the required software. Another advantage of this approach is that, if one does not have the software multiply routines, there is less software to be debugged, and no possibility of interrupts or other microprocessor features interfering with the timing of the multiply routine.

The main thing to remember is that hardware can often do the task more easily and less expensively than software. It is also advantageous to use hardware to simplify software. If software is simplified, its overall cost may decrease enough to economically justify using a more expensive hardware approach. The old idea that anything can be accomplished through the use of software is not economically valid.

CODING THE PROGRAM

Program in Modules

Assembly-language programs can often become so complicated that they are nearly impossible to decipher. What is needed is some type of organization and logical structure in the program itself. One approach is to write programs as modules.

A large assembly-language program could thus be broken up into a number of smaller program modules. The code residing in each module would then be a short, logical, self-contained section of the major program. Typically you would break a large program into logically self-contained subsections.

An example might be a program that inputs data from a keyboard, processes this data, and then passes it on to a printer. The program would be subdivided into one section that deals exclusively with the keyboard, another section that analyzes and processes the data, and a third section that controls the printout of this data. Each section would be a separate program module. Each program module would be assembled separately from the other modules. Inputs to and outputs from each module would be carefully defined to allow these modules to talk to each other. One module would contain only the keyboard-handling routines; a second, only the data-analysis routines; and third, the printer and the method by which data is passed to it.

The reason for this task breakdown is simple: small, independent modules are much easier to design and debug. Programming in independent modules, you are less likely to make mistakes about how various pieces of your program will interact or communicate. Since each program module in your system has an independent definition, it can be worked on by different programmers if you are short of time. (See Chapter 4 for a more detailed description of task decomposition.)

Another good reason for programming in modules is that small, independent program modules may be shared or traded between different projects. A decimal-to-binary-conversion module could thus be used in your present project and in several future ones. This feature of program modules helps you avoid writing the same piece of code over and over again. Program modules written by other programmers can also be used by you. As long as the modules are well defined and somewhat generalized, they can be used for a very long period of time.

Use Header Blocks

One very important thing that every assembly-language program module needs is a header block. A header block is a collection of information about the particular program module it precedes. Header blocks should give the programmer enough basic information about the module to understand its purpose and see what changes have been made to it, and when.

A typical header block might be divided into three separate sections. The first section would be a system descriptor block; the second, a change list describing what changes were made, and when, to the module; and the third, a logical description of the module in pseudocode.

The descriptor block (see Figures 7-1 and 7-2 on pp. 113 and 114) gives the programmer enough information about a particular module to understand its function and basic input and output requirements at a glance. This header block should contain the following:

1. Program name
2. Version number
3. Date of the last program edit
4. Mechanism by which this module is invoked
5. Inputs and outputs used by the module
6. Function of the module
7. A note section for special remarks

The change list of module history (see Figure 7-3 on p. 114) is a very important part of a header block. The module history should contain enough information to allow the programmer to determine what changes have been made to a module, and when. Typically this section will contain three pieces of information:

1. Date the change was made
2. Version number of the program module at this time
3. An English-language explanation of the addition or change

The pseudocode block, (see Figure 7-4 on p. 115) is simply a logical explanation of what the module is supposed to do. Pseudocode is an English-language programming shorthand, a method of putting flow charts into English. This block should give a logical description of all operations taking place in the program module that follows it. Pseudocode will be discussed in much more detail in Chapter 4.

Comment Your Program

It would be very difficult to imagine a program that had too many comments; most programs have far too few. Everyone seems to agree that well-commented programs are a good idea, but in practice few people bother to comment their own programs. Excuses for not commenting a program range from the extra typing involved to the disk space required.

Comments explain what is going on in the program. For assembly-language programming, a good rule of thumb is that comments should appear on nearly every single line of code. There are two basic types of comments: some are used after assembly-language code to explain what is being done in the program; others explain what information is passed to a small task or subroutine and how the latter operates. This second type of comment is usually found in a small block ahead of the task or subroutine.

Comments should not be used to give a tutorial in assembly-language programming. Some programmers insist on commenting programs in this fashion:

```
MOV      A,B           ;move B into A
```

This type of comment is completely worthless. It is assumed that everyone reading this program knows assembly-language programming, so there is no need to teach such programming through comments. A better way to comment a program is to explain what the program is doing, and why:

        MOV   A,B   ;move count of keys input into accum.

This second comment speaks for itself. If a program is poorly commented, the person reading through it will eventually ignore those comments entirely, and so miss the few good comments in it. This would defeat the whole purpose of putting comments into the program.

Use Good Mnemonic Names for Variables

Understanding what an assembly-language program is doing is difficult at best. There is no need to further complicate the program and your understanding of it by choosing names for variables and subroutines that have no meaning. Bad examples of mnemonic names abound. Imagine a motor-control subroutine responsible for turning a motor on and off. If you call the subroutine ROBIN, and for other internal labels in it use EGG, BLUE, and NEST, will you remember what this routine does in three months? And will anyone else be able to figure it out? Such labels can only confuse anyone attempting to read the program.

A better choice of a name for this subroutine might be MOTOR. If the routine is relatively short, its internal labels might be MOTR10, MOTR20, MOTR30, and so on. The first name tells everyone that this routine has something to do with controlling a motor, while the other three inform the reader that these symbols belong to the MOTOR subroutine. Thus all these labels help identify the code they precede as belonging to the MOTOR subroutine.

Choosing good names for programs and variables is not that difficult. Usually program names are limited to six characters. Very expressive names can be made up of only six characters. It is not that hard to think of abbreviations for longer words and thus conform to the six-character rule. One of the most important things to do when choosing names is to be consistent. If you are consistent, anyone should be able to understand your labels with a little effort. This will help the general understanding of your program.

Program names must also be related to the program function. Examples of related program names include:

MOTOR Motor control subroutine
KEYIN   Keyboard input
DISK   Disk drive control routines
BINHEX Convert from binary to hex

Further labels within a routine should be composed of four-character abbreviations followed by a two-digit extension. If, for example, the major label is called BINHEX, then the other labels in this routine would be BNHX10, BNHX20, BNHX30, and so on.

Variable names should be chosen in much the same manner. Keep the variable names down to six characters in length. This can be done by eliminating vowels in favor of consonants. A motor-control flag, for example, might be called MOTRON, which stands for motor on, or MOTFLG, which stands for motor flag. This variable would contain the present status of a motor as a true or false value. Again, in choosing variable names, be consistent in both the manner of name selection and the techniques used for abbreviation. The name should generally represent some physical thing.

Be Consistent

One important characteristic of a good program is its ability to be understood not only now but next week and next year. Even with good documentation, a program needs other features in order to be understood at a later date. It needs to be consistent.

There are several ways to make a program consistent. One of these is the way in which mnemonic names are chosen. How are the labels for this program chosen? Is the abbreviation consistent throughout the program? Are module names chosen in the same manner from week to week and year to year? Are all RAM variables named in the same fashion?

Another area where consistency counts is program organization. All program modules should start, proceed, and end in the same manner. Just as books and documents have a beginning, a middle, and an end, so should each program module. This organization should stay consistent from week to week and from year to year.

A third area for consistency is programming style. The techniques which the programmer uses to construct programs should remain consistent from module to module and from system to system. New techniques should not be used in one module and then forgotten in the others.

The final area requiring consistency is documentation, which should be written in the same manner for each program module in a system. Unless you invent some great new documentation feature, your documentation should be consistent from system to system. To be consistent in your documentation style, you must first consistently document your programs.

Good program documentation should include header blocks in front of all program modules. Comment blocks should proceed each subroutine and explain its function. Code lines should also be commented. A manual is also needed to explain what is going on in each program module and how these modules interact. Following these guidelines for each program you write will lead to consistent documentation.

The major reason for being consistent in program names, organization, style, and documentation is simply to aid yourself. A program that is consistent throughout will be easier to debug. A well-organized program will be much easier to maintain and change. All programs have some life span throughout which they must be maintained. Since quite often it is up to the program author to see to this, why complicate your own job? Only a few weeks after a program is written, it may be difficult to remember what is going on in it and why it was done this way. A well-organized program can eliminate such problems.

Avoid Unnecessary Jumps

It would be difficult to imagine an assembly-language program that had no jumps or branch instructions in it. There are, however, many examples of programs that have far too many jumps. Too many jumps can make it very difficult to understand what the logic in the program is doing. There is a middle ground for the use of jumps in assembly-language programming. It is not necessary to completely eliminate them from your program or, on the other hand, to put in more than are absolutely required.

One type of assembly-language statement that uses jump instructions is the IF statement. Typically a program will contain logic such as: if this, then do Y, otherwise continue. Many programs handle this type of logic by testing for the condition and then jumping out of the main loop. Control is then passed to a small routine that performs function Y. After this routine is finished, it jumps back to the end of the IF statement. This type of programming involves the use of more jump instructions than are really necessary, and also makes a program hard to read. An example of this type of programming is:

```
            MOV    A,C            ;get character to compare
            CPI    TEST1          ;if equal do TEST1
            JZ     DOTST1         ;go to DOTST1
CKTST2:     CPI    TEST2          ;otherwise if equal to
            JZ     DOTST2         ;TEST2 go to DOTST2
EXITST:     INR    A              ;then add one
            MOV    C,A            ;save result
            RET                   ;and exit

DOTST1:     ADI    5              ;add five in this case
            JMP    CKTST2         ;and return

DOTST2:     SBI    3              ;remove three
            JMP    EXITST         ;and return
```

There is an easier way to do this type of logic function. Instead of jumping out of the main line of the program when a condition is met, jump around the code to handle that condition if it is not met. In this style of programming you place your program code in line. The following example shows how to use this technique:

```
*****************************************************
*  CHECK CHARACTER PASSED IN C AGAINST        *
*  TEST1 AND TEST2.  ADJUST IT BASED ON       *
*  THESE VALUES.                              *
*****************************************************

            MOV    A,C            ;get test character
            CPI    TEST1          ;if not equal to
            JNZ    CKTST2         ;TEST1, skip next
            ADI    5              ;else add 5
```

```
CKTST2:   CPI   TEST2      ;if not equal to
          JNZ   EXITST     ;TEST2, skip next
          SBI   3          ;else remove three
EXITST:   INR   A          ;add 1 on exit
          MOV   C,A        ;save result
          RET              ;and exit
```

This technique uses less jump instructions than the first example. It is easier to read, uses less memory, and also has fewer labels. Reducing the number of jump instructions has made this code more readable and easier to understand.

Avoid Tricks

At one time a number of programmers considered programming tricks an important part of microprocessor software. There were many excuses for the use of these tricks in programs. Some people thought that program memory was expensive, therefore it must be conserved. Others wanted their program to run as fast as possible. Some programmers simply wanted to be sophisticated. All these excuses were just that. Programming in assembly language is difficult enough without further complicating it by tricks.

Microprocessor memory becomes less expensive with each passing month. In just a short period of time we have seen EPROM memory chips grow in size from 256 bytes to 32 kilobytes. The price has also dropped proportionally as these chips grew in size. RAM memory has also become inexpensive in exactly the same manner. These decreasing memory costs have made the use of programming tricks that save a few bytes unjustifiable.

Another reason for using programming tricks was to save two or three microseconds of processing time. But there are now multiple versions of most popular microprocessors ranging in clock speeds from one to 12 megahertz. It is much easier to choose a faster microprocessor than to complicate your software with programming tricks. There is also a great deal of specialized hardware that can be used to reduce processing time. It is rarely necessary to worry about saving two microseconds of processing time. When a programmer must worry about such small amounts of time, he is probably better off considering an entirely different approach. Software should rarely be stretched to its very limits. Programming tricks should be avoided at all costs.

Programming tricks should be avoided for another reason as well: debugging a program filled with them can be nearly impossible. Programming tricks by their very nature are hard to understand, therefore they complicate your program. Complicated programs are difficult to debug. Another problem with debugging programming tricks is that they are difficult to remember. Two months after one has been written, it may be hard to remember how it was supposed to work.

Because of their very nature, programming tricks are difficult to fully understand. A trick that seemed to work perfectly today may turn out to have some hidden problem associated with it. This problem may not show up for several weeks or even months after the portion of the program that the trick is located in has been debugged.

One final reason for avoiding tricks is quite simple: if everyone uses tricks, sooner or later you will end up debugging someone else's trick. Most programmers have a hard enough time understanding their own work, let alone another programmer's trick. Avoid using tricks, if at all possible.

Build in Debugging Aids

Every program that is to be used must be debugged. Often the debugging process can take longer than the actual design and coding of the program. A large number of programs are never fully debugged. One way to decrease the amount of debugging time is to build debugging aids into your program.

Several debugging techniques are commonly used with assembly language. You can leave blank areas inside your program so program patches can be placed there. Also, you can make sure that all subroutines have only one entry point and one exit point so that, when a subroutine is debugged, only one breakpoint is needed to trap the routine upon its completion. This technique will be discussed in greater detail in Chapter 7.

For microprocessor systems another type of debugging aid can be easily implemented. Most microprocessors have some type of hardware associated with them that they control. By writing a maintenance routine, the programmer can easily debug the physical hardware and its controlling software before attempting to debug the logical section of his program. A maintenance routine can be designed that will exercise all the inputs and outputs under the control of the microprocessor. Not only can these routines be used to debug the initial hardware and software, but they can also be offered as a feature of your new product. They provide diagnostic or maintenance functions to the end user.

Another debugging technique for microprocessor-based systems is to design test software for your system. Quite often microprocessor systems will need some type of physical inputs that are too complicated to simulate in hardware. One way around this problem is to build special software that simulates the hardware input. This software is a diagnostic or test software routine for your system. You use one piece of software to test another.

Other types of test software include programs that pretend they are in charge of other program modules. This type of routine is used to test other program modules. It fakes all inputs to the modules that it controls, then monitors and verifies the results coming back from modules under its control.

Start Simply and Work toward the Complex

Debugging a microprocessor-based software product can often be a difficult task. Not only is it necessary to debug your software, but usually there is also new hardware that must be debugged at the same time. It is difficult to determine if your software is defective, when you don't know if the hardware is functioning correctly.

One solution to this problem is to code the simple routines first. The first thing to code might be the output routine for our microprocessor. Once this routine is coded, it can be used to debug the new hardware. Since this program is relatively simple, it is easy to debug in parallel with the hardware. The next step might be to code and debug input routines, starting out as simply as possible, so as to make it easier to debug two things at once.

This process ensures that you start simply and establish exactly what portions of your hardware are functional. While debugging these initial routines and hardware, you also get a good feeling for the operation of the new microprocessor system. This feeling will help you in your debugging when the program modules become more complex. You are also getting familiar with the uses and idiosyncrasies of this particular microprocessor development system.

DEBUGGING THE PROGRAM

Hand-Check the Program before Running It

Checking out a program module for the first time can be a very difficult task. Common errors can greatly complicate the debugging process. These simple errors should be caught before any attempt is made to debug the program. It is a waste of effort to debug errors that can be easily caught in some other manner.

There are several types of errors that can easily slip through an assembler. Once these errors have made their way into your program, they will be difficult to detect. Errors of this type include transposing characters, leaving out whole lines while typing, and typographical errors that assemble without any error message. There is no reason or need to debug this type of error with the rest of your program, since a simple hand check of the program can catch 95% of them. A hand check involves reading through the software at your desk before attempting to debug it. Typographical errors can be found fairly easily by this process.

Missing code can also be found this way. It is easy to skip over a line of code while entering a program. If you are rotating the accumulator left four times, it is all too easy to skip one rotate command in your typing. Likewise, missing increments to pointers can be found this way. Reading through the program will detect most of these errors, and the amount of time so spent will almost always be less than the time needed to debug such errors.

One final thing to look for are logic errors. Often simple logic errors are readily apparent when reading through the code and so can be corrected before you start the debugging. A similar type of error involves code that a programmer simply forgot about. You can easily forget to set a flag or do some other special task. A reading of the program can catch this type of error as well before the debugging begins.

Write Down Test Procedures

A major difficulty in debugging most microprocessor programs involves the test procedures used. Often it takes several hours to think up a procedure to test a new program module. Once you have decided how to go about checking out a program, the actual debugging time may be relatively short. Problems can occur later on, however, when a module you thought debugged turns out to have a bug in it.

It then becomes necessary to retest that particular program module. First you have to figure out how to test it. If you haven't written down your original test procedure, you will have to figure it out again. But if you have the original test procedure written down, you can often discover how this particular bug slipped through your debugging without your having to retest the entire module. At the very least, you don't have to reinvent the entire test procedure.

Check the Program in an Orderly Manner

Some programmers use the best possible structured techniques and top-down design to construct their programs. Once they have their programs designed and coded, however, they bring their programs up under the in-circuit emulator to see what doesn't work. This is the worst possible approach to debugging a microprocessor program. It is unreasonable to expect to debug a program all at once when that program is 12K long.

Microprocessor programs can be debugged in the same modular manner in which they were written. There is a structured approach to debugging programs. The structured approach to microprocessor programming differs from that for minicomputers and mainframes. In microprocessors it is important to ensure that the hardware environment you are working in functions correctly before most of the actual software debugging takes place.

To make sure the hardware is functioning correctly, it will be necessary to utilize some special software to test the hardware. Usually such software can be the basis of your hardware control module. There should be two specialized program modules, one to control all the hardware outputs and the other to control all the hardware inputs. These two modules are each used separately to test the microprocessor hardware environment and ensure that the outputs and inputs are working. A further check should be performed on memory. All microprocessor RAM and EPROM should be tested to verify that they are working correctly, before any other attempt is made to debug software.

Once the microprocessor hardware environment has been verified, a structured approach can be taken to debugging the rest of your software system. Software can be debugged module by module by going either from the more complicated control modules down, or from the simpler modules up toward the logic control modules. The important idea is to debug the software module by module, not as a whole. Program modules will aid in this process since they are logical, self-contained tasks that have simple, well-defined outputs and inputs. Thus it should be relatively easy to fake inputs into each program module and verify the outputs of that module.

Develop Debugging Software

Often it is necessary to develop specific software whose sole purpose is to debug other software. Well-defined program modules can often be totally debugged in this manner. If a software module is treated as a subroutine with certain specified inputs and outputs, it is usually not very difficult to create a control module. This control module will fake all the inputs to the program module under test and then verify the outputs from the program module. This type of debugging software can greatly speed up the total task of debugging your system. Each individual software module can be tested independently of all the rest. When all the program modules work independently, they can be put together to be tested as a system.

There are other types of debugging software that can help your design work, as for example software for debugging hardware. You could write memory test routines that read, write, and verify RAM in your microprocessor. This type of software can be used to verify that the new hardware design is correct or that new hardware boards are functioning correctly.

Other types of software might be written to simulate various types of hardware inputs to your system. Certain types of hardware inputs may be difficult to duplicate simply. Often the actual hardware for your system may not be available, which creates a testing problem.

An example might be a set of data that is supposed to arrive over a UART. While it is possible to verify that the hardware for the UART is working correctly, the device that is sending the information to that UART may not be available at that time, or may send data so fast that you cannot examine it. One way around this problem is to build a software module that simulates information coming into that UART and simply stores it away in the same manner that the UART control module does. This secondary module can thus be used to test all the rest of the data processing in your system.

These types of test software modules can be of great help in debugging your software. They can test software that is difficult to debug in any other way, and can also help debug your hardware. The time spent in coding these modules can be much less than the time spent in debugging without such aids.

3
Top-Down Program Design

The previous chapter was a general guide to programming in assembly language. Programming tips and techniques are quite useful, but for the most part they are based on coding a program. Before the actual coding of a program begins, it is necessary to have some type of program design. Very few people are capable of sitting down and writing a program without first thinking that problem through. Even if you are able to write a program without a design, you must admit that carefully designed programs tend to work better and take less time to debug than those written without a design. How then do we go about designing a program? Are different techniques available for designing programs specifically for microprocessors?

Over the years a number of program design techniques have been discovered that work quite well for minicomputers and mainframes. These techniques are used to break a large problem down into a number of smaller subproblems. This chapter covers the top-down design technique, and modifications that adapt it to microprocessors. These adaptations are needed because of the hardware-oriented environment that microprocessors run in.

PROBLEM SOLVING AND PROGRAMMING

Before going on to the actual program-design techniques, let us say a few words about problem solving. Solving a problem and writing a program are two very different things. In solving a problem you must define first the problem and then a solution. Programming is concerned with the implementation of that solution to the problem. Programmers who confuse problem solving and programming typically end up with very poor designs for their systems. They are more interested in implementing a solution than in finding it.

Just as it is not a good idea to sit down and code a program at a terminal, so it is not a good idea to sit at your desk and write code without a program design. It is very hard to solve a problem while you are busy implementing the details of a program. Wouldn't it make more sense to get a definition of the problem first, followed by a definition of the solution?

Problem Definition

The first step in solving a problem is to define it. Quite often microprocessor projects are poorly defined at the start. The first step in defining the problem is to understand what the product is supposed to do. What is the purpose of this product and how will it operate? The product could be anything from a microprocessor-controlled blender to a sophisticated accounting system. The important thing is to understand what the product is supposed to do. What comes into this system and what goes out? How does the operator interact with this device?

The easiest way to get all the information needed to define your product is to ask questions. Typically, specifications supplied for a product do not cover everything the product must do and all its possible modes of operation. It is up to the programmer to ask questions and thus define the product. During this process the programmer should be looking for logical contradictions in the proposed operation of his machine. This will help prevent faults in the system design. Quite often different features of a new device will conflict with one another. These conflicting features must be discovered as soon as possible and be either eliminated or changed. Once the programmer has a complete definition of what the device is supposed to do and how it is supposed to operate, he is ready to begin the next step of system design.

The system or device description should be written down in English. An English definition of the problem is necessary to make sure you have a complete understanding of it. If you can't write out an explanation of what a device is and how it works, how can you expect to write a program to do those functions? This definition also serves another purpose. A programmer usually makes numerous decisions on how a device will operate while doing his design. Once all these decisions have been written down, they can be presented to the people in charge of the product or to those who will use it. This ensures that your proposed solution is acceptable. Nothing is worse than completing a project, only to be told that it needs an additional feature or must have some features removed. You are looking for outside input on your proposed system design.

Problem Solutions

After going through all these steps to define a problem, it is time to start defining the solution to that problem. The solution will usually involve some type of program design. One of the best techniques for program design is called top-down design. The next sections of this chapter will discuss top-down design, and the modifications to this technique that are needed for microprocessors.

TOP-DOWN DESIGN

Breaking Down the Problem

Top-down design is an extremely useful technique for developing a program design. The basic concept of top-down design is quite simple: you approach the problem as a whole and divide it into smaller and smaller portions. The theory is that the smaller a program is, the easier it will be to design, write, debug, and maintain it.

One example of this technique could be the design of a complete accounting package. The first step in a top-down design — assuming we have a problem definition — is to separate the accounting package into smaller, more manageable pieces. It might be divided into three subtasks: accounts receivable, accounts payable, and general ledger. Next, each one of the three tasks would be further subdivided into separate sections or modules. This process continues until a given task can no longer be profitably subdivided. (See Figure 3-1 for an example of this process.)

During this task-decomposition process, it is important for the programmer to ignore the details of programming. He should not be concerned with the details of how the individual modules will work. The concern here is to divide the large program into smaller ones and to define how these modules interact with one another.

Decomposition of a problem

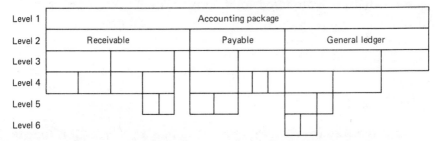

Figure 3-1. Decomposition of a problem. A complicated problem is broken down into smaller and smaller pieces. In this case the accounting package is broken into three sub-sections. Each of these pieces is then broken down again and again, until the problem can no longer be subdivided.

Module Restrictions

During the process of task breakdown you will have to consider how these modules interact. There must be some form of communication among various program modules, yet it is very important that this be kept to a minimum. The more links or communication between modules, the more likely it is that changes to one module will affect another. Also, the more complicated the communication between modules, the more likely you are to make an error in passing that information back and forth. Each program module should be a small, independent task with clearly defined communication lines to other modules. This communication should be held to a minimum.

Since program modules are supposed to be small, independent tasks, it is important to limit the physical size of these modules. With rare exceptions an assembly-language module should not exceed six to seven pages. (See Chapter 6 for a detailed explanation of program module length.) If a process cannot be solved in that many pages of code, it is too complicated and should be broken down into simpler pieces. This limitation in size ensures that the modules will be self-contained and address only one idea or program topic at a time. The small size makes these modules easier to code, debug, document, and maintain.

Module Hierarchy

In breaking a large problem down into smaller, simpler ones, the programmer is attempting to construct a program module hierarchy.

Program module hierarchy chart

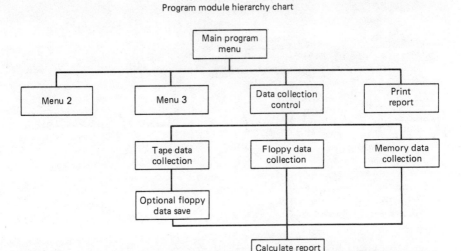

Figure 3-2. A program module hierarchy chart. A program module hierarchy chart shows the relative order of importance of the program modules that make up your system. A given module may only call or use other modules that are at a lower level.

This program hierarchy is simply an ordering of the program module's relative importance. During the breakdown process the programmer should construct a chart that shows the relative importance of each program module. This chart is called a program module hierarchy diagram. As seen in Figure 3-2, program modules of a given level can only call or invoke other program modules that are at a lower level on the chart. This helps to keep your program logic straightforward.

Data Flow

At the same time that you are breaking your problem down into smaller and smaller pieces, you should also be working on a data-flow diagram. This diagram is a drawing of how information travels through a system. Every computer program processes some type of information: data comes into it, is processed, and goes out of it. The data-flow diagram is designed to keep track of how this information flows through the system. This diagram, as shown in Figure 3-3, is concerned not with how information is processed, only with where it is going.

Data flow diagram

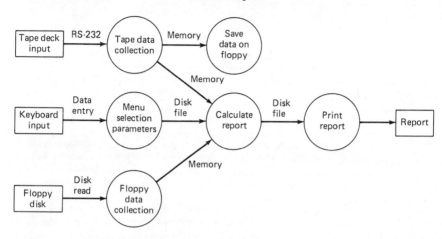

Figure 3-3. A data-flow diagram.   A data-flow diagram shows how information travels throughout a system. Data comes into it, is processed, and leaves it. The sources of information, the method of data transfer, and the type of data processing are all noted on this chart.

These two techniques — data-flow diagrams and problem decomposition — are the basic tenets of top-down design. There are, however, certain problems in using the top-down design technique on microprocessors. This technique was developed for minicomputers and mainframes, which have one strong element in common: the hardware environment they operate in is completely defined. The hardware on these types of computers does not often change and has previously been set up. This means that you are designing programs for a static, previously defined environment. Furthermore, the processing power of these computers can be considered limitless. Microprocessors, on the other hand, do not have infinite resources or predefined hardware.

Difficulties with Top-Down Design

What kind of problems will you run into if you apply the top-down design technique to microprocessors? One of the first problems you will encounter has to do with the use of microprocessors in the real world. A large percentage of the microprocessor systems developed are designed to be products. They are not used for basic computing, but for intelligent control of some device or product. A major problem in working with a product or device is that, at the same time the system design is going on, the hardware design for that product should be going on also. In most programming applications, the hardware design is scheduled to be completed concurrently with the system design. Program coding is not usually started until some hardware has been developed. Using the top-down design technique, you will run into a major problem. When the entire top-down design is finished, you are ready to define the hardware necessary to implement this solution. Unfortunately, it takes a fair amount of time after the hardware is defined, before you can have a working microcomputer system. Thus the major problem with top-down design is the need of a hardware definition for the system long before the design is finished.

A second problem with the top-down design technique has to do with the microprocessors resources. These resources are not infinite and in fact are often not very large. The programmer is forced to design his system within very fixed limits. These limits may include program size, amount of data storage available, speed at which the program must run, or amount of hardware needed to construct the system. Thus the top-down design technique has some problems when working with the fixed resources of a microcomputer. These design techniques must be modified to work within the limits imposed on microprocessor systems.

Another problem with the top-down design technique is that, in microprocessors, hardware often influences how data flows throughout the system. Hardware-software trade-offs are quite common in microprocessor systems. A simple example is found in a system that needs to perform basic arithmetic calculations. In doing a straight top-down design, you would design an arithmetic module to do these calculations. Once the system design was done, you would code the program and eventually produce this module. No thought would be given to the fact that there are single-chip hardware devices which would do the arithmetic functions for you. There should have been some way to evaluate the economies of purchasing this chip versus writing the software. This example demonstrates how the hardware features of a system can influence the system design. The top-down design technique does not take advantage of the adaptability of microprocessor hardware.

A TOP-DOWN, BOTTOM-UP DESIGN
FOR MICROPROCESSORS

The previous section discussed the top-down design technique and the problems associated with using it on microprocessor-based systems. Top-down design does not include hardware as part of the solution to a problem. With modification to the top-down technique, you can take the hardware environment into account. A top-down, bottom-up design technique has been developed for microprocessors. This technique takes hardware into account as part of the design process. It also attempts to provide a working hardware definition for your system before the system design is complete. This helps ensure that the microcomputer system will be ready for testing when the system design is complete. The following sections discuss this new technique and how to use it on a practical system.

Similarities between Techniques

The top-down, bottom-up design process starts out in the same manner as the older top-down design. The first thing to do is to define the problem. This includes:

1. Get a good understanding or feel for what your product is supposed to do.
2. Ask questions about the basic system operation.
3. Look for logical contradictions in the system operation.
4. Write a description of the problem in English.
5. Make sure that your definition is correct.

Once the problem is properly defined, the programmer can start defining the solution.

The next step in our modified design technique is to work on a program module hierarchy chart. You must break the large problem down into small, independent subproblems. In the top-down, bottom-up design technique you are not interested in getting a complete module description, as you would be in the top-down design process. You are interested only in obtaining a generalized module hierarchy. This chart is going to help you understand how data flows and is processed throughout your system.

While working on the program module hierarchy chart, you should also be working on a data-flow diagram for the system. This diagram· is a very important cornerstone in the top-down, bottom-up design technique. The programmer must track all data inputs through the proposed system. He should indicate how data is processed or changed from one form to another until some final result is obtained.

The end result from the module hierarchy and data-flow diagrams is two separate pieces of paper containing diagrams. With the help of these diagrams, the programmer will then start working from the bottom up to do the hardware design for the system. These two charts also make a good addition to the documentation for the system.

I/O Determination

By using the data-flow diagram, the programmer can construct a diagram that shows all inputs and outputs for his system, as seen in Figure 3-4. Using this new chart, he or she can determine exactly how much hardware is necessary to input all data and send out all responses. At the same time, the information this system will handle can be subdivided into its various types. This should give you a fairly complete accounting of how much parallel and serial I/O will be needed to make this system work. It should also help account for

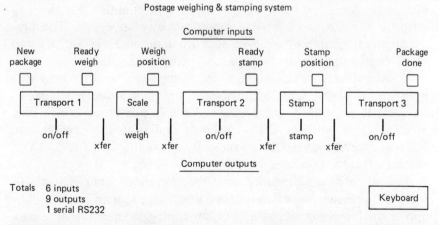

Figure 3-4. A postage weighing and stamping system. This diagram is constructed to determine exactly what types of and how much computer I/O is needed for a system. All inputs, outputs, serial lines, and other special computer hardware that the system will need are noted here.

how many counters, timers, multipliers, and so forth will be needed. The end result of this step is to produce yet another chart that shows how many input bits, output bits, serial channels, and other hardware devices will be needed to make the system work.

Memory Determination

The next step in this design process is to decide how much EPROM and RAM are needed for the system. Most microprocessor products cannot afford to leave large amounts of extra memory space unused, since this extra memory costs money and thus increases the cost of each individual device. A good estimate of the amount of EPROM and RAM needed is required before the program is designed and coded. This will allow the hardware design and construction of the microcomputer system to be started in parallel with the software design. Generally, the most difficult thing is to estimate the total amount of EPROM space needed. It is very hard to estimate program length when you have only data-flow diagrams and program module hierarchy charts.

Four basic techniques can be used to estimate total program length. The first is experience: programmers experienced in writing microprocessor programs can usually estimate, with a fair degree of certainty, how long a program will be. This method involves estimating the length of each individual program module. It is easier to estimate the length of a small module than a large one. The programmer can estimate how long each small module will be, then add these lengths together to derive a total program length.

A second technique involves the comparison of the proposed program with one written previously. Program modules similar in function to the ones you are writing can help you estimate how long your program will be. Often products similar to the one you are designing are already on the market. By examining these devices you can get a feel for how long your program will be.

A third technique involves using the amount of time available to write the program to determine how long that program can be. With only a small amount of experience, most programmers can develop a feel for how many lines of debugged code they can write per hour. If the programmer then feels that a given program can be written in one month, it is no problem to calculate the number of lines of code this will involve. From the number of lines of code, one can calculate the number of bytes of EPROM needed.

The final technique involves a simple guess at the total program length. While it may seem that this technique would not work too well, it is used quite often. Typically the guess is backed up by a special hardware function. The hardware will include a feature that enables the programmer to switch to a larger version of EPROM without redesigning the hardware, if he runs out of memory space. The hardware can be set up so as to adapt with minimum effort between 2716, 2732, 2764, and 27128 EPROMs. This can give the programmer up to eight times as much storage space as originally called for.

Once the total EPROM space has been determined, it is time to calculate how much RAM is needed for your system. Determining the amount of RAM space needed is not as difficult as figuring out how much EPROM is needed. Typically you must first determine how much, if any, specialized RAM will be needed. This would include any large data-storage requirements not normally found in a program. Once the specialized RAM amount is determined, the total RAM area needed is easy to calculate. In most assembly-language programming a ten-to-one ratio of EPROM to RAM can be used. But this ratio does not include any specialized RAM storage. To determine the amount of RAM needed, then, divide the amount of EPROM you will be using by ten and add in any specialized storage requirements. If a program is to be about 10K in length, 1K of RAM will probably be sufficient. Exceptions to the ten-to-one ratio include programs written under a real-time executive (which usually require a six-to-one ratio) and programs written in a high-level language.

Expansion Requirements

In the two previous steps you have determined how much I/O and how much memory will be needed for your design. The next step is to determine what the future expansion requirements of this system will be. These requirements also involve some thought about the economy of the system. How much extra memory and I/O space can be included with each system sold? If the number of systems sold per year is small, then a large amount of extra memory and I/O can be included with each. If, however, ten thousand units a year are to be sold, then each extra input bit's cost will be multiplied by that amount, severely limiting your system expansion ability.

The easiest technique used to figure expansion capabilities for EPROM and RAM involves including hardware provisions to switch among various memory devices. This allows you to expand memory without a great deal of hardware cost. A system might be designed to use 2716 or 2732 EPROMS. Starting with the 2716, you can double the memory space by simply moving to the other chip and making a minor hardware modification. RAM expansion may be handled in the same way. There are even RAM devices that are pin-compatible with EPROM. With a good hardware design you could even trade RAM for EPROM space.

Input and output expansion capability is often difficult to estimate. Most microprocessor products start out with some spare I/O. By the time these devices reach production, a great deal of this spare I/O has typically been used. The amount of spare I/O to initially provide depends upon several factors. The number of devices sold per year will greatly affect this amount. Generally, the more units sold per year, the less spare I/O will be provided. Also relevant is the function the device will perform. Devices that perform process control will usually have much more spare I/O than an individual product.

In any microprocessor design, remember to include *some* spare I/O. During the initial stages of a design it is frequently difficult to estimate exactly what I/O will be needed. Typically some new input or output requirement will crop up that needs a new I/O line. If there is no spare I/O, the hardware for the system will have to be redesigned, which may cause serious project delays.

Additional Thoughts

Another consideration in the future expansion process has to do with speed. If the process that the system is to control is near the limits of what that particular microprocessor can do, it would probably be useful to include hardware options to double the microprocessor's speed. Most microprocessors have several different versions ranging in speed from slow (1–2 megahertz) to fast (6–8 megahertz). By using a faster version of the same microprocessor, you can increase the speed of your entire system while adding only a modest cost to it. This extra speed may be needed in future versions of your system. As time goes on, microprocessor systems seem to grow or; more and more features are added, but rarely is anything removed. Each new feature eats up processing time and may eventually overburden the system. Providing for a future change in processor speed will allow more features to be added to a system without the need to redesign the hardware.

A final thought on future system expansion has to do with any new requirements that a device or product might need. For example, the initial design of a microprocessor system may give no thought to the addition of a printer. However, that idea may have been in the back of someone's mind. If this thought is not discovered before the hardware design is complete, it will be difficult to implement. It would be easier to include a little extra hardware in the initial design, so as to allow the system to utilize a printer at a later date. The actual hardware to implement this feature could be left off the microprocessor system until this feature is wanted. This will save money, but still allow the feature to be added at a later date. Considering the future requirements of a system can avoid serious changes to system design.

The next step in our top-down, bottom-up design is to make up a set of I/O charts showing all input and output information for a system (see Figure 3-5). This chart should define the following items:

1. Signal name
2. Type of signal (input, output, serial)
3. The address and bit where the signal can be found
4. The logical state of the signal for the program
5. The logical state of the signal for hardware
6. The physical point where this signal enters or leaves the microprocessor system (connector number and pin)

SIGNAL	DRIVER/RECEIVER	CONN. PIN	HWRD TRUE	PROG TRUE	BIT	PORT	
Display select 3	A2-10 8226	J1-34	1	0	7	E4H	
Display select 2	A2-13 8226	J1-36	1	0	6	E4H	O
Display select 1	A2-3 8226	J1-38	1	0	5	E4H	U
Display select 0	A2-6 8226	J1-40	1	0	4	E4H	T
Display data 3	A1-3 8226	J1-42	1	0	3	E4H	P
Display data 2	A1-6 8226	J1-44	1	0	2	E4H	U
Display data 1	A1-13 8226	J1-46	1	0	1	E4H	T
Display data 0	A1-10 8226	J1-48	1	0	0	E4H	
Block on light	A6-11 UHP-508	J1-2	0	1	7	E5H	
Uncouple	A6-8 UHP-508	J1-4	0	1	6	E5H	O
System reset	A6-6 UHP-508	J1-6	0	1	5	E5H	U
Auxil. reset	A6-3 UHP-508	J1-8	0	1	4	E5H	T
Lift pos. 1	A5-8 7407	J1-10	1	1	3	E5H	P
Lift pos. 2	A5-11 7407	J1-12	1	1	2	E5H	U
Dro pos. 1	A5-6 7407	J1-14	1	1	1	E5H	T
Drop pso. 2	A5-3 7407	J1-16	1	1	0	E5H	
Keyboard strobe	A3 Header	J1-32	0	0	7	E6H	
Key switch 1	A3 Header	J1-30	1	1	6	E6H	I
Key switch 0	A3 Header	J1-28	1	1	5	E6H	N
Keyboard data 4	A3 Header	J1-26	1	1	4	E6H	P
Keyboard data 3	A3 Header	J1-18	1	1	3	E6H	U
Keyboard data 2	A3 Header	J1-20	1	1	2	E6H	T
Keyboard data 1	A4 Header	J1-22	1	1	1	E6H	
Keyboard data 0	A4 Header	J1-24	1	1	0	E6H	

Figure 3-5. Main computer board configuration. This is a sample page from the I/O chart. It shows everything there is to know about the I/O signals listed: signal name, source, destination, and logic levels.

Speed and Interrupt Requirements

The next step in your design is to consider the system's speed of response. Most microprocessor systems must deal with at least some of their inputs in real time. When an input signal comes into the system, some type of response must happen within a fixed period of time. Even an accounting system is expected to keep up with keyboard input and produce records within a reasonable amount of time. Microprocessor-controlled devices such as blenders, microwave ovens, and video tape decks have very limited amounts of time in which to perform their functions. Thus the software design process must consider whether the proposed microprocessor system can respond quickly enough.

A decision must be made whether and where to use interrupts to speed up the response of your system. Certain inputs will require a response within a fixed amount of time. If this time is very small, interrupts may be required to ensure that the software can respond quickly enough. To determine if software can be used instead of an interrupt, you can calculate a simple software loop to handle that input. If the smallest possible program loop to handle that input is not at least 25% faster than needed, then the software loop will probably not function correctly; an interrupt would be a better way to handle the signal.

Another use for interrupts can be found in safety features. A microprocessor-controlled blender might have some type of safety shield associated with it. If the shield is raised, a switch closure will occur. The microprocessor must shut off the motor when this happens. Often the safety input will be run to a nonmaskable interrupt, to ensure that the blender will be shut down whenever the safety shield is raised. There is a problem with this use of interrupts, however. In a safety situation you should never assume that your computer will always correctly answer an interrupt. If the microprocessor fails right after turning on the motor, interrupts will have no effect. You should always back up safety features with hardware. The safety shield should be connected to the nonmaskable interrupt and to a cutout switch on the motor. Backing up the safety feature with both hardware and software helps ensure that at least one side will disable the motor.

Yet another use for interrupts is to place certain software routines in the background. The programmer can construct interrupt-driven routines that essentially run themselves. When an interrupt occurs, the processor stops what it is doing and performs the function associated with that interrupt. The rest of the program does not have to concern itself with the interrupt's function, which helps simplify the software.

A typical example of a background routine might be a UART handler. Suppose information is being typed on a keyboard and then processed by a microcomputer. It would be easy to construct an interrupt-driven UART handler. This program would respond to characters as they are typed on the keyboard. The interrupt routine would collect characters and save them in a buffer until it received a carriage return. Only then would this information be passed to other routines in the system. In the meantime the rest of the system need not concern itself with whether a character is ready at the UART. By placing this routine in the background, you make the rest of your program simpler. Putting things that are time-dependent or I/O-dependent into the background makes your program easier to follow, understand, debug, and maintain.

One final thing to consider when using interrupts is timing skew. Many times a very fast response to an interrupt is needed. This is typically a consideration in process control. Problems can arise when interrupts are used to provide very quick responses to input signals. The amount of time it takes a given microprocessor to answer an interrupt will vary. Most microprocessors answer interrupts at the end of the current instruction cycle. Since instruction cycles vary in length, the amount of time needed to answer an interrupt will also vary. Thus on a Z80 microprocessor with a two-megahertz clock, response to an interrupt can vary from instantaneous to 11.5 microseconds. Whatever function the interrupt performs must allow for up to 11.5 microseconds of variance from the time when the interrupt actually occurs.

If the process you are trying to control cannot tolerate this much timing skew, it would be best to replace the interrupt with some type of hardware. Another approach would be to use a faster version of this microprocessor. A four-megahertz Z80 would have a timing error ranging from zero to 5.75 microseconds.

Accuracy

One final consideration in the bottom-up portion of our top-down, bottom-up design has to do with accuracy. In the initial design of your system, some thought must be given to how accurate it should be. Accuracy means different things for different types of products or devices. In a process-control environment, accuracy tends to relate to the speed of response of your system. In a mathematical or calculation environment, accuracy has to do with the number of bits used in your calculations. Both types of accuracy can have a big influence on your system design.

In the control case a fast response to a large number of signals might require a faster microprocessor than originally thought. It might also affect the software design. The overall complexity of your software might have to increase, to provide the necessary extra speed. In a mathematical case, increasing the number of bits in a calculation increases the complexity of the software as well as the amount of data storage needed. Furthermore, larger numbers imply that the calculations will take longer. If there are a great number of calculations to perform, the processing time might become excessive. This would necessitate a change in the hardware design to include a hardware math processor. Thus system accuracy requirements can affect the system design by changing both hardware and software design.

Completing the Design

Once your hardware environment is designed, you have finished the bottom-up portion of your design. Now it is time to return to the top-down section and conclude it just as in a normal top-down design for a mainframe or minicomputer. The generalized program module hierarchy chart must be completely filled out. All program modules and their interconnections must be completely defined. Program module descriptions must also be completed at this point.

Once the design is finished, it is time to move to the coding process. Chapter 4 covers structured programming for assembly language and microprocessors. These structured techniques serve as a complement to the top-down design techniques discussed in this chapter. Both chapters will help you to produce well-designed, structured programs. These programs should be modular and easy to understand.

4
Structured Programming

Structured programming has been touted as the greatest boon to programming since the invention of high-level languages. It is supposed to offer great improvements over any other method of programming. However, it seems that relatively few people are using these techniques on microprocessors. Programmers, who often use assembly language, feel that structured programming techniques will not work with this language, so they have no reason to learn these techniques. This chapter will inform you otherwise: structured programming techniques work nearly as well in assembly language as they do in higher level languages.

Most programmers who have not been exposed to structured programming feel that these techniques merely involve the removal of the jump instruction. Their logic then goes: since I'm working in assembly language, I can't avoid jump instructions. Therefore, structured programming won't work for me. Some programmers also feel that it is much harder to program in a structured fashion. They dislike all the restrictions and new rules that they must learn.

Structured programming is a valid technique for working in assembly language. There are many solutions to the various problems raised in discussions about why structured programming and assembly language won't mix. The advantages found in the structured programming techniques are so numerous and so useful that it would be much to your advantage to learn them. Your microprocessor programming can be greatly advanced by the addition of structured programming techniques.

STRUCTURED PROGRAMMING TECHNIQUES

To adapt structured programming to assembly language, it is first necessary to understand precisely what this entails. Structured programming is much more than just the removal of all jump instructions. It involves a set of rules and restrictions that force a structure or organization on your software. If you force organization on your programs in a consistent and thorough manner, your software becomes much easier to read, understand, and debug. It will also be much harder to make a logic error when using these techniques. Structured programming also forces you to simplify your programs.

Three Tenets of Structured Programming

The most basic tenet of structured programming is that any program that can be written for a computer can be written with just three basic tenets or structures. The first tenet is the sequence or order in which instructions are executed. A program will always be executed in a certain order, one statement following another. The second tenet is the ability to do conditional programming. This typically involves an IF/THEN command: if something is true, then do the following function; otherwise, do a different function. The third tenet is the WHILE/DO command, which gives you the ability to repeat a sequence of operations any number of times: while some variable is less than x, continue doing the following function.

In-Line Code

Structured programming involves considerably more than writing programs using only these three basic tenets. Another condition of structured programming is that all programs should be written in a straight-line sequence. Programs or modules should be written in a simple, straightforward, single-line manner. All IF statements should work in-line. You should not write an IF statement that jumps out of line on one condition to perform some special function. Everything must follow in a straight-line, logical order.

```
                    USE

          LDA    COUNT      ;get the count of keys
          CPI    5          ;if > = 5 then
          JGE    BYPASS     ;skip on
          MVI    B,0FFH     ;otherwise set B=FFH
          MVI    C,'5'      ;and C= ASCII 5
BYPASS:   CPI    10         ;now check count > 10
                            ;program proceeds normally
```

```
                    NOT
          LDA   COUNT      ;get the key count
          CPI   5          ;if count < 5
          JLT   ADJUST     ;then go to adjust
RETURN:   CPI   10         ;otherwise proceed
                           ;on with program


ADJUST:   MVI   B,0FFH     ;set B=FFH
          MVI   C, '5'     ;and C= ASCII 5
          JMP   RETURN     ;go to main line of program
```

Program Module Limitations

Another fundamental rule of structured programming has to do with tasks. Any task or subroutine must have only a single entrance and a single exit. In assembly language it is quite common to see a subroutine that shares an ending with some other subroutine. This should not be done in structured programming. When two subroutines share a common ending, serious problems can arise when changes must be made in one of the programs: changes to the first subroutine may affect the operation of the second, owing to the common piece of code they share. Thus structured programming prohibits subroutines or tasks from sharing portions of their code. However, this does not prohibit them from both calling the same subroutine to perform some task; they just are not allowed to share code.

The one-input and one-output rule forces another change on assembly-language programming: you should not use conditional returns in a subroutine. Conditional returns imply that a subroutine has more than one exit point. This in turn makes setting up breakpoints and debugging that module much more difficult. All conditional returns should be replaced with conditional jumps or branches to a common exit point. At this common exit point there will be one return instruction.

```
                    USE
CHECK:    MVI   C,BAD      ;set bad flag
          CPI   80H        ;if < 80H
          JLT   EXIT       ;then say bad
          CPI   0A0H       ;if > A0H
          JGT   EXIT       ;then say bad
```

```
          ANI    1              ;if odd
          JNZ    EXIT           ;then say bad
          MVI    C,GOOD         ;otherwise – good
EXIT:     RET                   ;common exit point

                 NOT
CHECK:    MVI    C,BAD          ;set bad flag
          CPI    80H            ;if < 80H
          RLT                   ;exit
          CPI    0A0H           ;if > A0H
          RGT                   ;exit
          ANI    1              ;if odd
          RNZ                   ;exit
          MVI    C,GOOD         ;otherwise set good
          RET                   ;and exit
```

The reason for this rule is quite simple. If some change must be made in the way this subroutine exits, for instance setting a flag, it is easy to accomplish if there is a common exit point, whereas multiple exit points render this type of change difficult. If you overlook a single conditional return in your change, you have introduced a very subtle bug into your program.

Another rule concerning tasks or subroutines has to do with how they communicate with each other. Structured programming requires that communication between any two programs be kept to a minimum. This applies equally to subroutines, program modules, and tasks. When writing your programs, make only weak connections between programs. By reducing the amount of communication between modules, you reduce their interaction. (See Figure 4-1 for good and bad module communication.) Limited interaction reduces the effect that changes to one module may have on another.

Structured programming also requires a process called task decomposition. The whole program must be broken down into smaller and smaller pieces so as to make the programming task easier to accomplish. This process is much the same as that performed in top-down design: there, you construct a program module hierarchy chart; here, you are breaking a program down in the coding aspect. The program module hierarchy chart and data-flow diagram can help you in this task. You must break all complicated programs down into smaller, simpler tasks provided with only one entry and one exit

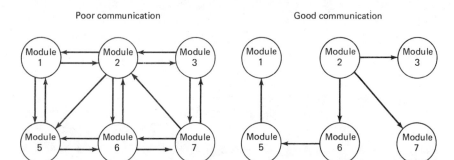

Figure 4-1. Module interconnections.   Broad communication paths between individual modules defeat the purpose of individual modules. They can also lead to serious errors in your programs by propagating errors from module to module.

point, and designed to minimize intertask communication. Figure 4-2 shows an idealized example of the structured attack on a programming problem. You start with a goal derived from your design and proceed until the program is coded.

STRUCTURED ASSEMBLY-LANGUAGE PROGRAMMING

Avoid Excessive Jumps

How do you adapt structured programming to assembly language? Most assembly-language programs use numerous jump or branch instructions. The conditional jump instruction is used to make decisions throughout a program. How can you get along without these jump commands? There are three different ways to do this.

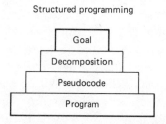

Figure 4-2. Structured programming. A programming problem can be worked out in a series of steps. You begin with a simple statement of the goal or problem you seek to solve. This statement has few details. As you proceed from goal to decomposition to pseudocode to program, you add more and more detail. By the fourth level the program is completely coded.

The first way is simply to reduce the total number of jump or branch instructions in your program. Typically, assembly-language programs can be written in several different ways, some using more jump instructions than others. The method that uses the least amount of jump instructions will give you the closest approximation to structured programming. The following example shows two different ways of coding a program; the second method uses fewer jump instructions.

```
                              USE
        MOV    A,B            ;get test character
        CPI    80H            ;if not equal 80H
        JNZ    CKTST2         ;skip next
        ADI    10H            ;else add 10H
CKTST2: CPI    0A0H           ;if not equal to
        JNZ    EXITST         ;A0H skip next
        SBI    5              ;else subtract five
EXITST: MOV    B,A            ;save result
        RET                   ;and exit


                              NOT
        MOV    A,B            ;get character to compare
        CPI    80H            ;if equal do TEST1
        JZ     DOTST1         ;go to DOTST1
CKTST2: CPI    0A0H           ;otherwise if equal to
        JZ     DOTST2         ;A0H go to DOTST2
EXITST: MOV    B,A            ;save result
        RET                   ;and exit


DOTST1: ADI    10H            ;add 16 in this case
        JMP    CKTST2         ;and return


DOTST2: SBI    5              ;remove three
        JMP    EXITST         ;and return
```

Reducing the number of jump instructions helps to order your programming. The only exception to this has to do with the single exit point from a subroutine. All conditional returns should be replaced with conditional jumps to a common return.

The second way to eliminate jump or branch instructions is easy to implement; it involves the use of macros. (For the programmer who is not familiar with macros, Chapter 6 has a detailed description of what they are and how to use them.) A good assembler will allow the programmer to construct several different macros to aid in his structured programming techniques. It is possible to construct IF/THEN/ELSE and WHILE/DO macros for assembly language. These macros will use jump instructions internally, but while using them you do not have to concern yourself with what code is being generated. As far as you are concerned, you are not using jump instructions, since they appear internal to the macro. These macros can give you much of the power of a high-level language, yet you still have access to all the features of the assembler. A number of programs can be written solely with these macros. No jump instructions would be needed. If a program calls for the use of jump instructions, just keep them to a minimum. The following example shows the use of WHILE and WEND macros in assembly language. For more information about macros, see Chapter 6.

Macro Definitions

WHILE	MACRO	X, VARIAB,COND,WHAT	WHILE macro definition
WHIL&X	LDA	VARIAB	; \ test
	CPI	WHAT	; *for
	J&COND	$+6	; / conditions
	JMP	WEND&X	;if not met – quit
	ENDM		;end definition
WEND	MACRO	X	;WEND definition
	JMP	WHIL&X	;loop indefinitely
WEND&X	EQU	$	;exit label
	ENDM		;end of macro

= =

Using the Macro

FLASH:	WHILE	1,LITCNT,LT,20	;while count < 20
	CALL	WAIT	;wait 1 second
	CALL	LITEON	;turn light on
	CALL	WAIT	;wait another second
	CALL	LITEOF	;turn light off
	WEND	1	;end WHILE loop
	RET		;exit subroutine

There is a third method for reducing the total number of jump instructions in a program. Conditional calls can be used to replace large numbers of conditional jump instructions. Conditional calls perform the same function as conditional jumps, with the added feature that they return to the same point, thus keeping your programming closer to the in-line form. The conditional call can be used to test for some operation. If the test is successful, then program control will be transferred to the subroutine that handles this function. Upon completion, the subroutine will return control back to the main-line program.

```
        LDA    FLAG       ;get flag to test
        ORA    A          ;set processor flags
        CNZ    HANDLE     ;do routine if not 0
        LDA    DONFLG     ;check to see if done
        ORA    A          ;set the flags again
        CZ     NOTDON     ;do NOTDON if not done
        .
        .

HANDLE: MVI    A,5        ;routine to handle
        .                 ;process is just
        .                 ;an ordinary subroutine
        RET               ;ends with a return
```

Structured Assembly-Language Rules

So far, most of the discussion on structured assembly-language programming has centered on reducing the number of jump instructions used. This makes structured programming look as if it is concerned only with jump instructions, which is not the case. Structured programming is interested in imposing a specialized order on software. To impose this order, programs should follow these rules:

1. Minimize the number of jump instructions used.
2. Program in modules — small, self-contained, independent tasks that perform a single function.
3. Limit communication between program modules.
4. Ensure that each program module, task, or subroutine has only one entry and one exit point.
5. Limit interactions between program modules.
6. Do not use conditional returns.

7. Keep assembly-language modules less than seven pages long.
8. Try to keep programming in a straight-line fashion.
9. Let no program or subroutine share code with any other program or subroutine.

By using all these techniques, you can generate tightly structured assembly-language code. The addition of macros to your programming can also help structure your software. These techniques, when used with the top-down, bottom-up design mentioned in Chapter 3, will have a major impact on your software. Used together, they should speed software development time, reduce errors, and produce well-designed, well-defined software.

Pseudocode

Another technique to help you in your structured assembly-language programming is the use of pseudocode. As the name implies, pseudocode is an imitation programming language — a simple English-language form of flow charts, consisting of statements invented by the programmer. It might look like this:

DO WHILE MOTORS ARE TO BE TURNED ON

    GET A NEW MOTOR TO TURN ON

    IF MOTOR IS ON AND LIGHT IS OFF
      TURN ON LIGHT
      SET FLAG TO INDICATE LIGHT ON
    OTHERWISE
      SEND ERROR MESSAGE TO SCREEN
    ENDIF

    IF MOTOR IS OFF AND LIGHT IS OFF
      TURN ON MOTOR
      TURN ON LIGHT
      SET FLAGS TO INFORM SYSTEM
    ENDIF

END DO WHILE

Why invent a new programming language that has to be translated into assembly language? There are several good reasons. First, it is hard to totally apply the structured programming techniques to assembly language, owing to the nature of the language. This technique gives you an intermediary language that is more structured in style.

Second, this technique provides a logic flow chart of your program. If this pseudocode is located in a header block (see Chapter 2), each program module will contain its own flow chart, which makes debugging and understanding the program easier.

Third, assembly-language programmers frequently make mistakes in implementing the details of a program. With a written explanation of the program, it is much more difficult to make this kind of mistake. This technique ensures that you have worked out the details of your logic before implementing a solution.

Benefits of Structured Programming

Structured programming imposes a number of rules and restrictions on your assembly-language programming. What benefits can be expected to offset the extra work that structured programming seems to require? There are four major benefits that can greatly help you in writing your programs.

The first benefit is very important. By using structured programming techniques, you will reduce the number of logic errors in your software. Assembly-language programming is typically quite complex. Since you must handle all the details of programming yourself, it is very easy to get lost in the details and forget the whole. Any technique that reduces the number of logic errors can greatly aid the programmer. By reducing the number of logic errors, the programmer can be assured that the amount of debugging time will be reduced. Structured programming reduces the number of logic errors by forcing a tight organization on your programs.

The second benefit is a more readable program. Because of the order imposed on your program, your software becomes more readable and easier to understand. Convoluted logic is much harder to write in structured programming, because of the restraints and organization imposed on your program. The program is also written in an in-line fashion. This too helps in making the program readable. Making a program readable gives you an advantage when it is time to debug and maintain your software.

The third benefit is a reduction in the time needed to debug your software and to make changes in it. Structured programs are easier to understand than nonstructured ones. Any program that is easier to understand will be easier to debug. Structured programming minimizes communication between modules. When you are debugging, this reduction in communication makes errors easier to locate and fix. There will be fewer complicated intermodule errors. In the same manner changes are easier to implement, since a change to one module is less likely to affect another unrelated module.

A final benefit from structured programming is an increase in programming productivity. With a little experience, it is easier and faster to write structured than nonstructured assembly-language code. This type of programming helps the programmer to think in a more logical manner. The module communication restrictions help you to break your programs down into small, self-contained tasks, which eases the chore of assembly-language programming. All these factors make you more productive.

Why should you care about being productive? Most programmers work for a company, and companies typically reward more productive employees with money, which is one good reason. Another reason is that quite often there isn't enough time in the day to do all the required work. Why not be a bit more productive and avoid working past five o'clock? Structured programming will not only ease your programming chores but also make sure that you get home in time to enjoy yourself.

POOR ASSEMBLY-LANGUAGE TECHNIQUES

Avoid Misuse of Instructions

Several programming techniques must be avoided when doing structured assembly-language programming. One of the most important things to avoid is misuse of the microprocessor instruction set. Steer clear of instructions that give you the result you want only as a by-product of some other operation. If 20 different instructions will clear the carry bit on your microprocessor, use only the simplest one. Using one of the other 19 instructions that happens to clear the carry as a side effect of its operation will only make your program confusing and hard to follow. Misuse of an instruction also makes a program very difficult to debug. When you read an instruction, assume it is put there to perform its main function, not its side effect.

Avoid Undocumented Instructions

Another misuse of microprocessor instructions is the use of undocumented operation codes. Several microprocessors currently on the market have instruction codes for which the result is undefined. A number of programmers were unsatisfied with this state of affairs and investigated these undefined instructions. They determined what these instructions did and then published the results of their studies. As a consequence there are now a number of programs that depend on these undocumented instructions. The problem with these new instructions is that they are not supported by the manufacturer. The design of a microprocessor can change at the whim of the manufacturer. The manufacturer only guarantees that the new device will meet the old specifications. The old specifications never said anything about those undefined instructions. Thus you may find that your program no longer works with the new version of the microprocessor.

Another problem has to do with second sourcing of microprocessors. Your undocumented instruction may work on the original manufacturer's micro, but what about other manufacturers' microprocessors? If a production run mixes the two different manufacturers' microprocessors together, does that mean that only half your systems will work? Avoid using any form of undocumented instructions in your programming.

Avoid Self-Modifying Code

A third thing to avoid is any form of self-modifying code. This type of programming is never a good idea: it is complicated, and is never really necessary to make a program function. Anything that can be done with self-modifying code can be done with normal programming techniques. The only thing that self-modifying code does is make your program more difficult to understand and much harder to debug. It increases the possibility of serious errors in your program and decreases your chance of fixing these errors.

Examples of the types of problems caused by self-modifying code are numerous. Suppose that a program using self-modifying code has been completely debugged. What happens when a new feature must be added to this program? Whether you or someone else implements this change, the results will probably be the same: you will not remember exactly how this special portion of code worked. You know it does its job, but you don't know how. So you add a new feature to the program and a major bug appears. Did you yourself add the bug, or is it a result of the self-modifying code? It will be difficult to find out, since you don't remember how the code works.

Even worse would be the case where you are maintaining someone else's program. It is hard enough to maintain and change an assembly-language program written by someone else; you don't need the added problem of self-modifying code. Avoid such code in all your programs.

5
Software Development

One important question that never seems to be asked is, where does software come from? Perhaps this is because everyone knows how software is produced. Yet most people have never seen a dedicated software development system, let alone an in-circuit emulator. There are a multitude of tools available to speed software development. This chapter will discuss these tools and how they are used to produce software.

It takes a fair amount of both hardware and software to create new software. Some type of computer system is needed to enter, store, assemble or compile, and test the program under development. While almost any computer can be used to develop software, there is a special class of computer systems that seems to be favored most by professional programmers. These systems differ from other computer systems in one or two major ways. First, they will always have some specialized software with which to debug a program. Second, they may also have a special piece of hardware to aid in software debugging.

The purpose of these two items is to ease the task of program testing. Once a programmer becomes familiar with this type of software and hardware, he will typically be hard-pressed to figure out how he debugged programs without them. These two items are very useful in the debugging portion of the software development cycle.

THE SOFTWARE DEVELOPMENT CYCLE

The actual process of developing software is quite straightforward. There are eight major steps. For most systems these steps must be followed in a linear fashion: you must complete step 2 before starting on step 3.

1. System design
2. Writing code

3. Editing code
4. Program assembly and/or compilation
5. Linking and locating program modules
6. In-Circuit emulation or program debugging
7. Final program checkout
8. Final documentation

System design is an important part of any software project. It typically takes up about 30% of the total project time, if done right. A top-down, bottom-up approach, as mentioned in Chapter 3, seems to work best in the microprocessor environment. It will save a great deal of time in the long run, if you do your system design before attempting to write any code whatsoever. The system design is concerned with determining a solution to a given problem.

Writing program code is the next step in software development. This step takes up about 15% of the project's time. When writing code you should be concerned with implementing a solution to a previously solved problem. In this portion of the software development cycle you are interested in solving programming problems. Writing code should be done on paper and *not* at a terminal. It is all too easy to make mistakes while writing program code. Writing program code directly on a terminal only increases the chance that you are going to make a mistake.

Editing code into your machine must be done next. As mentioned before, editing does not include any actual program coding. Editing usually takes up about 10% of a project's time. A good program editor can greatly speed up this process and eliminate some of the drudgery of typing. Very long programs can be entered in by someone other than yourself. Most professional typists can enter a program into your machine in half the time you would need.

Assembly of a program can be a time-consuming process. It will also inevitably turn up several typing errors. Correcting these errors will take time and require the use of the program editor. As you go through the software development cycle, you will notice that you keep ending up back at the editor. This is why a good editor is so important. You will spend a lot of time with it. Specialized hardware can speed up the assembly process. Most computer systems are faster than the printer attached to them, so a printer buffer can speed up assembly time. A quick survey of printer buffer users shows that addition of a printer buffer decreases assembly time by from 25 to 50%.

Linking and locating program modules is the next step in the software development cycle. This process will also discover errors that have to be corrected, so you will end up back with the editor program again. Typical errors involve symbols not being made public to other modules.

The next step — often considered the most difficult of all — is program debugging or testing. Program testing procedures will vary, depending on whether an in-circuit emulator is available. Whether it is or not, debugging will almost always use one program to check another. Some type of specialized program is necessary to enable you to trace and monitor your own program flow. Typically a debug program is used that allows you to step through your software in any manner you specify. The testing of a program (steps 4 through 8) typically takes the remaining 45% of a project's time.

Final program tests are a concept that many people do not understand. If a program has been thoroughly tested with an in-circuit emulator or a debug program, what can be wrong with it? The answer is — plenty! The problem with debugging your own software is that you wrote it and are thus thoroughly familiar with it. It is unlikely that you would abuse your software while testing it. The end user of your software is under no such restrictions. Thorough testing of software requires an independent party to do the final testing — someone unfamiliar with the software. A good choice would be either the night watchman or the president of the company. Either should be able to find plenty of problems you have overlooked. Another inherent software bug is the program that is impossible to understand or use. The president of your company is a good choice to locate this kind of problem, and he will see to it that the problem is corrected.

The last step in the software development cycle is the documentation clean up. Most of the documentation should be completed by this time. Header blocks and comment fields should be present in all programs (see Chapter 7). A good editor is now essential. Using it you can go through your program modules and collect all pertinent documentation. This can be put into a single file and sent to the printer. Note that most people don't leave much time, if any, for this step. Thus good comments in your program modules plus a good text editor will ensure that this step gets completed.

PROGRAM ENTRY

Program Editors

A large amount of your time is spent editing programs, therefore it is in your best interest to get the finest editor available. There are two basic types of editors. Older, more primitive editors are line-oriented and are compatible with a teletype. Newer editors are screen-oriented and act as windows into your files.

A line-oriented editor is not very easy to use. It treats your text file like a long series of lines of text. The editor maintains a pointer which indicates where it is working in the file. This pointer is not available to you. The only way to determine where you are working in a file is to instruct the editor to type out some of your text file. A typical editing session might have you move down 15 lines into your file, at which point you type out a few lines of the file to verify where you are. Having done this, you can insert some new text. Finally, you should print out the previously entered text to verify that no mistakes were made when it was entered. This involved process is the major reason why most programmers have switched to screen-oriented editors.

A screen editor functions as a window into your file. Imagine your file as if it were typed on a continuous piece of computer paper. A screen editor lets you move a window around on this paper. The window is typically 20 to 25 lines long by 80 to 256 characters wide. If you move your cursor up a line, the entire window will move up one line in the file. With this type of editor, you can always see what you are typing and where it is going.

A screen-oriented editor has a number of special features not found in a line editor. While some screen editors have special features not available in others, most good text editors have certain things in common.

A good editor should allow you to read and write alternate files from your program. When you are editing a file you should be able to instruct the editor to write out a portion of that file under another name — a great help in doing documentation. You should also be able to read in separate disk files into your program module. This allows you to take a standard header block from the disk (see Chapter 7) and place it at the beginning of each program module. You then need only add in the comments for that new file. This is much faster than typing in the whole header block for each new file.

Another useful feature goes by several different names. This is the ability to put deleted text back into a file. Essentially, the editor maintains a stack of deleted material. When you tell it to, the editor will take the last item deleted and place it wherever the cursor is pointed. To move a line of text, all you need do is delete the line, move the cursor to where you want the line moved, and pop it off the stack.

On occasion a program becomes longer than 80 characters in width. Either comments become too long or a table entry grows too big. The assembler typically doesn't care if the line is longer than 80 characters — after all, most printers have a 132-character width. However, a number of editors won't let you enter a line greater than 80 characters long, or they wrap this line around to the beginning of the next line. A good editor will allow you to enter a line of any width. It should simply move the entire screen window to the right when you are entering a long line.

Another useful feature is the ability to do block moves and block copies. Block moves are helpful when you must shift parts of a program around. Block copies are especially helpful when programming in assembly language. Assembly language can be very repetitive. It is often easier to duplicate one section of program and modify it than type it in for a second time. A good editor should easily support these two types of operations.

The last major feature of a good editor is the ability to execute macros, which lets you customize the editor to your own personal tastes. Macros can allow you to perform complex operations that are not possible without a large number of key strokes.

Some minor features are useful but not necessary, as for instance an editor that is designed for program entry, not word processing. It is also helpful if the editor is user-friendly. Finally, an editor should be easy to learn and use, since this makes your job that much simpler. Keeping key strokes to a minimum is one feature of this type of editor.

Operating Systems

A good operating system and its auxiliary programs can also speed up program entry. Such a system should support fast and simple disk transfers, since a computer is expected to perform its job quickly and reliably. The command to do a disk transfer should be simple and not ambiguous.

The operating system should support a good directory program. The directory program is the major way you keep track of your programs. It should display the date and time a program was created. This information is extremely helpful when backing up disks, or when more than one programmer is working on a project. The directory should support wild cards in its searches. Typical wild cards are * for anything and ? for any character. A command might look as follows:

DIR *.ASM

This tells the system to display all programs with the extension of ASM. It would also be helpful if you could request the directory to print all files not of some specified form. Finally, a good directory should be sorted alphabetically. Otherwise it is often hard to find a program in the directory, since the entries tend to end up in a random order.

A good operating system should also support fast and easy-to-use copy and backup routines. The copy routine should support wild cards and query you if the file to be copied already exists on the backup disk. Backup routines typically copy disk information track by track to speed up the copying process. They should also erase the backup routine itself from the newly created duplicate disk. This ensures that if you ever accidentally switch the disks around before making a backup, you will not lose all your work. In some operating systems it is possible to damage a disk directory, and once this is done a track-for-track disk copy preserves the error.

TESTING WITH A DEBUG PROGRAM

The Debug Program

Once a program is written and entered into a machine, it has to be tested. One of the two major ways to test a program written in assembly language involves the use of a debug program. A debug program is a simple piece of software that allows you to control the execution of another program. It provides you with a number of specialized features:

1. Multiple break points
2. Register display
3. Single-step capability
4. Symbolic debugging
5. Ability to assemble and disassemble code

Multiple break points are a very important part of any debug program. This feature allows you to start a program wherever you desire, and to stop program execution at any one of several places that you can specify. Essentially, the debug program starts your program up at the address you have specified and forces it to stop at the program break points you have likewise specified. When this feature is combined with the register display instruction, it lets you track and verify what a program is doing at all times.

Register display is also very important. Most of the action in a microprocessor takes place in its internal registers, so to effectively debug a program, you must see what is in those registers. The display produced by this command is specific to the processor being used. A typical display for an 8080 processor might look as follows:

A=xx CxZxMxPxIx B=xxxx D=xxxx H=xxxx SP=xxxx PC=xxxx where,

display	represents	range
A	Accumulator	(0 – 0FFH)
C	Carry flag	(0/1)
Z	Zero flag	(0/1)
M	Minus flag	(0/1)
P	Parity flag	(0= odd, 1= even)
I	Interdigit carry	(0/1)
B	BC register pair	(0 – 0FFFFH)
D	DE register pair	(0 – 0FFFFH)
H	HL register pair	(0 – 0FFFFH)
SP	Stack pointer	(0 – 0FFFFH)
PC	Program counter	(0 – 0FFFFH)

Register display commands are quite useful, but do have one major drawback: they tend to use the microprocessor stack to save the information from the microprocessor's registers. Normally this doesn't cause a problem. However, as single-chip processors become more popular, a number of people have run into the same special problem. A single-chip processor typically has a very limited RAM area, usually from 64 to 128 bytes. This RAM has a tendency to be used up quickly, so there is limited room for the program stack. If your program needs all the RAM and leaves only a small amount of room for the stack, you may find the debug program can overwrite your RAM! It is the debug program itself that puts too many items onto the stack and thus overlaps the stack and RAM storage.

The single-step feature is often used as a last resort in debugging a program. It allows you to step through your program instruction by instruction, displaying the registers with each step. This enables you to completely trace program execution, although at a much slower pace than normal. This slowed operation of your program may, unfortunately, cause it to not function properly since many programs are time-dependent. Such programs must operate at some minimum speed in order to keep up with external inputs or outputs.

Symbolic debugging is an important feature that you may not have been exposed to, unless you have already used a relocatable assembler (covered in much more detail in Chapter 6). Symbolic debugging implies that the symbols you used in writing your program are available while you debug it. Suppose your program began with the label START and ended with the label FINISH. A symbolic debug program would allow you to enter the following type of command:

GO FROM START TO FINISH
or
GO FROM START TO START+45H

instead of

GO FROM 07CDH TO 089FH

While this may seem like a mere convenience, it is actually much more. Relocatable assemblers do not give you a listing of your program containing absolute addresses. Without a symbolic debug program, you have no easy way to figure out where your program actually begins and ends. Chapters 6 and 7 will cover this in more detail.

The ability to assemble and disassemble code is a useful feature in a debug program. While not absolutely necessary, it can greatly reduce the amount of time it takes to debug a program. The disassembly feature allows you to check portions of your code to ensure that the assembly language statements are what you expect. The assembler feature allows you to easily enter patches into your program while testing it. It is usually more feasible to patch a program being tested than to stop and correct each error as it is found. Maintaining a patch list and correcting the errors only when they get too numerous is a common practice.

Testing under the Debug Program

Testing a program should be handled in much the same way as designing one — in a modular fashion. Organize yourself before you set out to test your software. Either a top-down or a bottom-up test procedure is preferable to attempting to debug an entire program all at once.

One good rule in testing software is to do more than just test a routine once. A single correct execution is no indication that a module will function correctly all the time. If possible, a routine should be tested by using every possible input. If this is impractical, the routine should be tested using minimum, maximum, and some statistically average inputs. This form of testing gives you a better chance of detecting subtle bugs and eliminating them from your final product.

Several kinds of initialization errors can be very difficult to detect. If you neglect to initialize a piece of RAM, your routine may check out correctly anyway. This can happen if the RAM your program didn't initialize just happened to be set correctly before your test began. Of course you can't count on this happening all the time. A debug program will usually let you fill all or part of memory with a given value. A good way to test a program is to start out with all memory set to 0AAH. If the program seems to run right, then set the memory to all zeros. If things still run well, try it again with memory filled with 0FFH. These tests will just about guarantee that you have no memory initialization problems.

One last type of initialization problem to look for involves hardware. Most microprocessor systems use some kind of specialized hardware. Usually these chips will automatically initialize themselves. Some programmers thus feel it is not necessary to initialize these I/O devices, but nothing could be further from the truth. While most of these chips are supposed to initialize themselves, they may not do so under all possible conditions. If the power reset circuit for your system is not quite up to specifications, the I/O chips may not initialize themselves correctly. If you also neglected to initialize the I/O device in software, your program will have an interesting problem. If you insist on programming in this fashion, you will end up with intermittent problems that can be impossible to locate. It pays off in the long run to initialize all I/O devices before you use them.

The assemble-code feature of a debug program can be quite useful in solving some I/O-device initialization problems. You can enter a small routine that initializes all I/O devices incorrectly and run this test program before you start your software debug cycle. Thus all hardware is set up incorrectly before your program starts. If your program doesn't initialize some piece of hardware correctly, you should be able to find it this way quite quickly.

TESTING WITH AN IN-CIRCUIT EMULATOR

As you have probably guessed by now, a debug program is of little use to someone developing software for a product that won't support that debug program. Suppose you are writing software for a tire balancer. It is unlikely that you will have a debug program or floppy disks for your new tire balancer. The software for the balancer will probably not run too well on your microprocessor development system. What you need is some way to test your software in the actual product you are working on.

There are two basic ways to do this. The first uses an EPROM emulator, a device that imitates an EPROM. You down-load your program into this device, which then plugs into your product in place of EPROM. It will give you basic debug capabilities in much the same manner as the debug program mentioned before. This type of device is usually less expensive than an in-circuit emulator, but has significantly fewer features associated with it. You pay less for it, but it makes your software testing more difficult than it need be.

The In-Circuit Emulator

The other major way to test software in your product is with an in-circuit emulator. This is a connection between your product or device and your software development system. An in-circuit emulator consists of some hardware that resides in or near your development system, and a cable that plugs into your product in place of its microprocessor. The major advantage of an in-circuit emulator is that it allows you to use the full resources of your development system in the debugging of your software. This device also supports a number of special features that can be accomplished only with hardware.

A good in-circuit emulator will provide a number of special features that are very useful in debugging software, but a bad one can make you tear your hair out. Beware of cheap imitation in-circuit emulators! A good emulator should have at least one microprocessor of its own. It should not use the development system's microprocessor to perform its emulation tasks. Some of the best emulators have up to four microprocessors, all dedicated to debugging your software. What do all these microprocessors do? Here is a list of features found in a good in-circuit emulator.

1. Multiple soft and hard breakpoints
2. Memory and I/O mapping
3. Register display
4. Single step
5. Symbolic debugging
6. Real-time trace of instruction cycles
7. Direct memory, register, and I/O control

At first glance, most of these features seem to be the same as in the basic debug program. There are, however, some major differences between these two ways of testing a program. Using a debug program instead of an in-circuit emulator is like using a bicycle instead of a high-performance sports car. You can probably get to your destination with either, but you will get there a lot faster and with a lot less hassle in the car. The same is true of a debug program. The larger and more complicated a program gets, the more likely it is you will *need* an in-circuit emulator.

Emulator Features

Using breakpoints with an emulator is considerably different from using them in a debug program. In a debug program, a breakpoint usually implies that software is stopped *before* a specified program instruction is executed. With an in-circuit emulator, breakpoints usually occur *after* a specified program instruction is complete: you can go until a conditional jump instruction is executed, and then see where the program is going to jump to! Breakpoints under an emulator are usually done with hardware, not software. Because of this, two different types of breakpoints are available. The basic type of breakpoint says, go from here to there and stop; this is a soft breakpoint. The other type — a hard breakpoint — says, go until the following instruction is executed and then, *without stopping the program,* put out a pulse which can be examined with an oscilloscope. This hard-breakpoint feature is very useful when debugging real-time software; it does not slow the program down.

Breakpoints are usually not limited to instructions. A good emulator will allow you to stop program execution after a specified RAM address has been read or written to. You can also break only if a specified value has been read or written to RAM. The same commands also apply to I/O devices. You can break when the microprocessor sends a character to the UART in your product. You should also be able to go until a specified instruction, RAM location, or I/O device has been accessed any number of times. These specialized breakpoints give you considerably more power than can be found in a debug program.

Memory and I/O mapping are features not found in debug programs. They can serve two basic purposes when you are debugging a program. Their simplest use is to specify what memory exists in your system. Suppose the product you are developing has memory ranging only from 0000H to 3FFFH. By using memory mapping, you can tell your development system that no other memory exists in your product. From that point on, the in-circuit emulator will not allow your software to access memory that is not in the map you have defined. The emulator will halt whenever your software accesses that memory. This is a handy way to catch several types of software problems. I/O mapping can be set up in the same way.

A different use for memory mapping is also possible. Quite often a product is designed to run a program from EPROM, which can create a problem in testing software. How do you down-load a program into a device that has very little RAM? If you put the program into EPROM – a lengthy process – how do you set break-points in it or patch it? Memory mapping lets you get round this type of problem. You can use memory mapping to tell your in-circuit emulator to utilize the RAM memory in your development system instead of the memory in your product. In our previous hypothetical example, a product had EPROM memory ranging from 0000H to 3FFFH. Through memory mapping techniques you can instruct the in-circuit emulator to redirect all memory access to those 4000H locations to some range of addresses in your development system. This allows you to load the program to be tested into RAM in your development system. Now you can bring the full power of your development system to bear on the software debugging task of another microcomputer.

Both register display and single stepping are available under an in-circuit emulator. While they may have more frills than their relatives in a debug program, they are basically much the same. Both single stepping and register display may be done with hardware in an emulator environment. This will probably not be noticeable to you, the user.

Debugging a program with all the symbols you created for it is a great advantage. While working under an in-circuit emulator, you can really take advantage of these labels. Suppose you have a problem with a subroutine common to a number of other modules. You can stop the program when a problem occurs in that subroutine, but then you need to determine the routine that caused the problem. With symbolic debugging techniques this is very easy to do. You need only instruct the emulator program to display things symbolically and then show you the contents of the stack. The emulator will look at each item on the stack, then locate the label closest to it. You will have an English-language label to tell you what module called this subroutine. A typical set of commands might look as follows:

```
BASE SYMBOLIC
DISPLAY STACK 3
    MOTRFG
    MOTCNT
    MOTOR+31
```

If your subroutine pushed two items on the stack, this display tells you all you need to know about what module called this routine. A flag and a count have been pushed onto the stack after the subroutine was called. The calling module used the symbol MOTOR 31 bytes before the subroutine was called. With this information you should be able to locate that module and start correcting the bug.

Real-time cycle trace is found only in in-circuit emulators. It won't be found in a debug program because it takes a fair amount of hardware to implement. A real-time cycle trace is a feature of an emulator that gives you the ability to display the last N instruction cycles of your processor. Typically you can see from 40 to 256 previous instructions. Suppose you set a breakpoint in your program, and when the emulator gets there it stops as instructed. What happens if you can't figure out how the processor got there or why it arrived in the state it did? The real-time cycle trace allows you to ask the emulator how the processor got there. The emulator will display the last instructions that the processor executed. Usually these commands will be displayed in assembly language, although some emulators display only in machine code. Seeing the actual program instructions executed, you should easily determine how and why your program arrived in the state it did.

Direct memory, register, and I/O control are totally software-driven features and thus could be part of either an in-circuit emulator or a simple debug package. For some unknown reason all three of these features are rarely found in debug packages, but are usually present in emulators. Simply put, these software features give you direct control over memory, processor registers, and input/output devices. Software commands will allow you to change the status of all these items at will.

The ability to change memory is quite useful. When program bugs are discovered, you can usually correct them with this feature. If you have forgotten a piece of code, you can add it in for test purposes. The ability to change memory is also helpful in checking for RAM initialization problems. A typical change memory command might look as follows:

CHANGE MEMORY 43FH = 0,0,56H

This command instructs the emulator software, starting at location 43FH, to change memory to the specified bytes. Thus three separate consecutive bytes will be changed.

Direct register control is another useful feature. While debugging, quite often you will reach a point in your program where a bug has made it pointless to test your routine any further. The bug has destroyed the contents of a register or set them up incorrectly. The register-control feature of your emulator can help you get past this impasse. It allows you to change the contents of any specified register. Thus you can set the registers up the way they should have been and then continue with your testing. A typical register control command looks like this:

CHANGE REGISTER A = 23H
   or
CHANGE DOUBLE REGISTER BC = 0FFFFH

Direct control over I/O ports is the last of these three features to discuss — and also the feature least likely to be found in a debug program. Yet this feature is at least as useful as the other two. The ability to change output ports or read input ports can be a great help. If your software is not reading an input port, it might be a good idea to check to see if that port is really working correctly. You can use the read port command to test the port. This ensures that a great deal of hardware is working correctly before you try to debug your software. A typical test might look as follows:

DISPLAY INPUT 13H
> 00H
- - -now hold down the switch in question- - -
DISPLAY INPUT 13H
> 04H
- - -the switch works!!

Control over output ports can be just as useful. You can use it to test control of hardware, just as you used the input command to test hardware. The output command can also be used to initialize hardware that needs special command sequences to be brought up. Normally UARTs need a series of commands to be sent to them in order to be initialized. The output command can be used to do this, if you are not sure how well your software is working.

CHANGE OUTPUT 34H = 01,01,04,56H,25H
- - -send an initialization sequence to a UART- - -

IF THE PROGRAM WASN'T TESTED WELL

Thorough testing of a program can be a complicated and time-consuming task. Time constraints often seem to force a less than thorough approach to software debugging. Rather than run five complicated tests on a program module, it is often easier to rationalize ending all tests after the third successful run of that module. After all, time is running short and the module passed the first three tests with flying colors. This sort of attitude can also lead you to include modules that haven't been tested at all. Suppose a system works well and a new module is to be added. Rather than go to the trouble of thoroughly testing that module and its interactions with the rest of the program, it is much easier just to see if the program as a whole seems to work. If it does, then the new module must be doing its job! Such an attitude can lead to serious problems, most of which won't show up for a great deal of time.

Locating a Problem

One major problem associated with inadequate debugging before a program is released, has to do with locating a software problem after it has been released to the field. No one has a perfect memory. The more time that passes between the writing and the debugging of a piece of code, the harder that debugging becomes. You will inevitably forget how a piece of code works and how it was designed. To debug that code, you must relearn that information. For a large program this can be a considerable task. The amount of effort originally needed to debug it has grown considerably for each day that has passed since it was written.

Another thing that is easy to forget is how a program was originally tested. Yet when you are called upon to locate a particular problem in software, it helps to know this. Often, knowing the symptoms of the problem plus the original testing techniques will be enough to locate a problem. This is because you can use the problem symptoms to see how the bug might have slipped through testing.

This book contains a number of sections on proper documentation techniques for assembly-language software. When you are called back to debug a program written two years before, you will quickly discover the worth of those techniques. A program lacking good documentation is going to be very difficult to debug later. The documentation that you wrote two years earlier will be a real help. Consider too the case where you are called in to debug someone else's software: without proper documentation, you are going to be at that task quite a while. Do yourself and others a favor by including a good set of documentation with each program module you write.

Problem Reporting

Another major problem with software that wasn't tested well has to do with error reports from the field. The amount and accuracy of information coming from the field about possible software bugs can make it difficult to determine if there even is an error. The amount of information about a possible bug may be totally inadequate to locate and correct a problem. Often the people supplying the information have little or no software training and can only report generalities. This makes your specific task of finding and fixing the problem difficult. At other times their information is quite correct, but if they had only noticed one or two more facts, you could locate the problem in minutes instead of months. If you thoroughly debug a program before it is released, you are a lot less likely to have to rely on someone else's reports.

The accuracy of information on software bugs seems to be inversely proportional to the reporter's involvement in other portions of the project that could also cause this type of error. Given a choice between doing some extensive field work to locate a problem or reporting a possible software bug, most overworked field service people will report the bug to you. That's human nature. There also seems to be a whole class of people who would rather redo something than fix it, which can cloud the accuracy of their reports.

Just sorting through problem reports can be a difficult task. Gathering the proper quantity of accurate information to identify a problem may not be easy. It might even require your presence in the field. While this may be one way to get that world tour you've been dreaming of, it probably won't be too much fun. Once again, the easiest way to avoid these problems is to do a better job of debugging your program initially.

Released Software Versions

One last problem concerns software that wasn't tested well before release. Every time software is released to the field, it should have a version number assigned to it, to make it possible to identify what version of software is being used at each software site. Without a software version number, it will be difficult to locate a reported problem. The problem report could concern a bug that has already been fixed everywhere but at the one site still reporting the problem.

Problems can also arise when there are too many versions of software in the field. If a given site has more than one version available to it, it will probably mix those versions up or combine them. This is particularly a problem when software is distributed in the form of EPROMs: invariably someone will mix EPROMs from version 1.3 with those from version 1.4, leading to some interesting problem reports. The only real way to avoid this problem is to boldly identify the software version on each EPROM and try to ensure you get all of the old version back.

Another problem also involves multiple versions of software. The more versions of a particular set of software that are created, the more likely it is that different sites will end up using different versions of the same software set. If a site that is using an older version of software complains about a bug or wants a new feature, it is possible you might fix the software for them only. This leads to two diverging sets of the same software. If you think it is hard to maintain and debug one piece of software, try it with two similar but not identical sets!

Software that is not well tested before its release will eventually have to be fixed. This will result in numerous version numbers for that software. Multiple versions of the same software will have numerous problems associated with their creation, tracking, and maintenance. Testing software well before its release can minimize these problems.

6
Using Your Assembler

RELOCATABLE ASSEMBLERS

Several features found in assemblers can greatly aid a programmer in producing software. One major feature to look for is the ability to create relocatable object modules. A relocatable assembler lets you create programs or sections of programs without regard to the actual location or arrangement that those programs will occupy in memory. Further, a program configured to run at one particular location may be easily changed to run at another location without being assembled again.

How does an assembler go about doing this? Every microprocessor has certain instructions that must reference where a particular symbol is located. An example might be a jump instruction: if the jump is absolute, the microprocessor needs an address to go to. (Relative jumps avoid this problem.) What can a relocatable assembler do about this type of address?

Relocatable Code

A relocatable assembler handles this problem in a simple manner. It marks every absolute symbol for future reference and ignores the fact that the symbol address does not exist at the moment. This means the output of a relocatable assembler is not pure machine code. The object files put out by this assembler need additional processing before they can be used.

Since additional processing must be done on relocatable object files, these assemblers come with one or two additional programs to do this processing. These programs are typically called linkers or linking locaters. The locater portion of the assembler takes in a starting address for the program and then goes through the entire relocatable object file, resolving all the absolute symbols. This process is extremely quick — much faster than assembling an entire program all over again. Thus the relocatable assembler puts out object files that the locater processes. If you move the starting address of a program, you need only run the locater to change your entire program.

If you look in detail at what features are available under relocatable assemblers, you will find some other useful functions. A large number of programs written for microprocessors are designed to run out of EPROM. Programs written for EPROM must have their data areas separated from their code areas and will also have a further subdivision of memory. Most microprocessors do not really care where in their address space a program is run. They do, however, care about a few special addresses such as interrupt vectors and power-up locations. So an assembler that produces relocatable code also has to be able to produce some absolute code.

Memory Management

A relocatable assembler typically has three (or more) different ways of dividing program memory: the code area, the data area, and the absolute area. This data area may be further subdivided, depending on the particular microprocessor (the 6800 has two types of data areas). A typical assembler would offer several directives that allow the programmer to specify which type of memory storage he would like. All relocatable assemblers give a programmer the ability to define memory in at least these three ways. These instructions might look like this:

```
          DSEG                  ;the following code goes into RAM
                                ;no address is needed by the assembler

FLAG:     DS        1           ;save one byte for flag
POINTR:   DS        2           ;save a pointer
          .
          .

          ASEG                  ;following code is absolute addressed
          ORG       0H          ;the assembler also needs an address

          JMP       START       ;jump from power up vector to start
                                ;of program

          CSEG                  ;the following code goes into EPROM
                                ;no address is needed by the assembler
```

```
START:    MVI       A,5           ;start of main program
          STA       FLAG          ;set start up flag
          .
          .
          END                     ;end of the program
```

This example shows the use of all three assembler directives. The DSEG command (data segment) tells the assembler that the following code will go into RAM. The starting address of this RAM will be given to the locater program, not the assembler. The ASEG command (absolute segment) tells the assembler that all further code must be assembled at a specific address. The CSEG command (code segment) tells the assembler that all further program code will go into EPROM. Its starting address will be specified to the locater in the same manner as the data segment.

Modular Programs

One attractive feature of a relocatable assembler is that it lets you subdivide a long program into several smaller and simpler modules. Smaller modules are easier to debug than a larger, more complex program. There is less possibility of creating a hard-to-find bug. A small program module will also assemble faster than a long one. The assembly time is determined mainly by the length of the listing sent to the printer. By keeping program modules short, you can significantly reduce the amount of time spent waiting for the printer.

What size should your assembly-language listing be? Most experts advocate limiting your listings to seven pages or less. Why seven pages? If you use the header block techniques described in Chapter 7, you will find they take up two pages on the average. This leaves you with five actual working pages for your listing. Each page should have a one-inch top and bottom margin, which leaves 54 lines per page. This gives you a total of 270 lines to work with. Good assembly-language commenting typically results in a two-to-one ratio of code to comments and blank lines. This turns the 270 lines of listing space into 180 lines of assembly-language code. Most experts agree that between five and ten lines of assembly language are equivalent to one line of high-level code. This implies that the 180 lines of assembly language are about the same as an 18-to-36-line program in a high-level language. So a seven-page assembly-language program is more or less equivalent to a half-page high-level language listing.

Another feature of modular programming is the ability to divide the software work between several programmers. After each specific section of a program is defined, other programmers may write those modules without interfering with your work. These modules may also be partially debugged on their own. It is much easier to debug many small modules than one large one.

To program in separate modules, the assembler must have some added features. If various separate program modules are to work together, they must have some way of referencing data and routines in one another. A relocatable assembler gives you a method for doing this with two special assembler directives: PUBLIC and EXTRN.

Label	Opcode	Operands
optional:	PUBLIC	list of symbols
optional:	EXTRN	list of symbols

The PUBLIC directive tells the assembler that you would like other program modules to be able to see and use this symbol: you are making a symbol public for all the world to see. An example of a routine that needs to make a symbol public might be a motor-control subroutine. Any module that needs to turn this motor on or off would call one subroutine to perform this function. Since the other program modules need to reference the subroutine name, you would declare this name PUBLIC as follows:

```
        PUBLIC  MOTOR
        CSEG
MOTOR:  DI                ;no interrupts allowed
        IN      MPORT     ;read the present port
        ORI     1         ;turn on motor bit
        OUT     MPORT     ;and send out port
        EI                ;interrupts ok now
        RET               ;end routine
```

The other new assembler directive is EXTRN, which stands for external. When you use the EXTRN directive you are telling the assembler that the following symbol is external to this program. A program module might need to turn a motor on by using the common subroutine MOTOR described previously. Since this program module does not actually contain the MOTOR subroutine, you would declare it external to this program. If you do not use this directive, the assembler would flag any subroutine calls with an error, because the subroutine address was not defined to the assembler. The following example demonstrates the use of the EXTRN directive:

```
        EXTRN   MOTOR        ;tell assembler this symbol
                             ;exists elsewhere
        CSEG

START:  MVI     A,TRUE       ;\
        STA     RUNFLG       ;/ set program running flag
        CALL    MOTOR        ;turn on motor
        LXI     H,TABLE      ;do something else now
        .
        .

        END
```

There is another advantage in using modular programs. Programs written in this fashion can be used for more than one job. An example might be a decimal-to-binary conversion routine. Why write the same routine for each new system? It would be much easier to define it as a program module and use the same module for each new system or job you work on. In this fashion you can create a library of standard software modules for common tasks. This library can greatly reduce the tedium of writing programs that must solve the same type of problem over and over again. Also note that a program module needs to be debugged only once; after it is in your library, it never has to be tested or fixed again.

Relocatable assemblers offer the programmer several very important features. Software can be organized into program modules with each module performing its own independent task. Program modules can be assembled separately and later linked together to form a complete program. Individual modules may also be tested independently. Finally, the complete program is relocatable: if the data memory or code memory hardware is changed, the program can be relocated in a short time without needing to be assembled again.

MACROS

Assembly language is a very powerful programming aid. It gives the programmer complete access to all processor features and hardware. Unfortunately, it also has numerous drawbacks. It is extremely tedious to program in assembly language, for the same lines of code keep appearing over and over again. A simple function may appear hundreds of times in a program. If that function takes three lines of code, the programmer will have to type and debug those same three lines over and over again.

Another problem with assembly language is its readability. Even with comments, header blocks, and module descriptions, an assembly-language program can be far from readable. If it is hard to read a program, it is going to be all the more difficult to debug it. Furthermore, a hard-to-read program will be very difficult to maintain.

A software tool that can help overcome these difficulties is the macro assembler. A macro assembler gives the programmer a special feature — the ability to create macros. In its simplest form, a macro is a way of telling an assembler to replace one piece of text with another.

A macro assembler has a special set of commands that allow you to define a section of text with a single symbol. Thus those same three lines of code that you previously typed in over and over again can be replaced with a single macro instruction. Once a macro is defined, there is no danger that a typing error will occur.

The easiest way to understand what macros are capable of doing is to look at a simple example. Consider the following program written in 8080 assembly language:

```
LOOP:   INX   H          ;point to next
        INX   H          ;double byte entry
        MOV   A,M        ;get byte from table
        RLC              ; \
        RLC              ;  \ swap 2 nibbles
        RLC              ;  / in accumulator
        RLC              ; /
        CPI   5          ;if A = 5
        JZ    FUNC1      ;go to function 1
        CPI   20         ;if A < 20
        JC    FUNC2      ;go to function 2
        CPI   45         ;if A > 45
```

```
        JZ      SKIP            ;go to LOOP
        JNC     LOOP
SKIP:   RET                     ;else end this routine
```

This small routine performs a simple function, yet it is tedious to write, and its function can easily be misunderstood. Consider the following routine written with macros:

```
LOOP:   INC      H,2                    ;point to next entry
        MOV      A,M                    ;get the number
        ROTATE   L,4                    ;swap the 2 nibbles
        IFA      EQ,5,GOTO,FUNCI        ;if A = 5 go to FUNCI
        IFA      LT,20,GOTO,FUNC2       ;if A < 20 go to FUNC2
        IFA      GT,45,GOTO,LOOP        ;if A > 45 go to LOOP
        RET                             ;otherwise end the loop
```

Even if one lacks an understanding of how macros work or how to construct one, this routine is easy to follow. It is closer to English than the same routine written only in assembly language. There are less lines of code, which makes typing mistakes less likely. Also, you no longer have to remember exactly how the 8080 flags are set after a compare. The macro can translate the LT and GT symbols for you. Finally, this routine is noticeably shorter than the first. Since most assemblers work only as fast as their printer will allow, the macro routine will assemble faster because it is shorter.

Macro assemblers were developed long ago for mainframe and minicomputers. Since macro assemblers were already in use when microprocessors were developed, almost all the macro assemblers developed for microprocessors follow the same macro definition and directive syntax. Some assemblers will limit the number of macro functions available or provide extra features, but they almost always follow the same syntax. The following paragraphs cover the definition and use of macros using Intel's 8080 assembler. As noted before, the use and construction of macros is nearly identical in most micro-processor assemblers.

Macro Definition

Before a macro can be used, it must be defined. Defining a macro is simply a way of telling the assembler what a particular symbol is going to represent. Like all statements in an assembly-language program, a macro definition must follow a certain syntax.

MACRO Directives

Label	Opcode	Operand
name	MACRO	optional variables to pass
– –	ENDM	– – – – – – –

A macro definition consists of at least two major pieces: a beginning statement and an end statement. The beginning statement must tell the assembler the name of the macro, while the end statement tells the assembler to end the definition of this macro. The following macro definition tells the assembler that a macro with the name TEST exists.

```
TEST     MACRO          ;this statement defines macro "TEST"
         ENDM           ;this statement ends macro "TEST"
```

This macro TEST is one of the simplest possible macros to define. It tells the assembler that the symbol TEST exists. It also tells the assembler that every time it sees the symbol TEST, it should replace it with whatever text was placed between the TEST macro definition statement (MACRO) and the TEST macro end statement (ENDM). There is no text between these beginning and end statements, so the TEST macro generates no code.

A slightly more useful example can help illustrate how a macro works. If you have ever programmed with the 8080 microprocessor, you probably noticed that there is no "clear the accumulator" instruction. One of the easiest ways to perform this function is to "exclusive-or" the accumulator with itself. Thus a typical 8080 program will have numerous XRA A instructions scattered throughout it. Each of these instructions is meant only to clear the accumulator, yet they don't say so. A macro could make your program much more readable by giving you a new instruction, CLEARA. This new instruction will really be an exclusive – or, XRA A. You are, in effect, renaming the XRA A command to make it more readable. The following definition creates the CLEARA macro:

```
CLEARA   MACRO          ;clear the accumulator macro
         XRA    A       ;exclusive or accumulator against self
         ENDM           ;end the macro
```

This macro tells the assembler that each time it sees the symbol CLEARA, it should replace that symbol with all statements found between the CLEARA macro definition and macro end. The assembler will replace CLEARA with the single instruction XRA A, as in the following example.

You Type

```
MOTOR:  CLEARA              ;clear the accumulator
        STA     MBUSY       ;set motor busy flag to 0
        .
        .
        RET
```

The Assembler sees

```
MOTOR:  XRA     A
        STA     MBUSY       ;set motor busy flag to 0
        .
        .
        RET
```

This example shows what the macro assembler does internally before the program is actually assembled. The assembler first translates all macros to assembly language and then assembles those statements. Typically the programmer is not interested in what code (in this case an XRA A instruction) is generated by a macro. He is more interested in having a readable program.

Passing Values into a Macro

While simple text replacement is a useful feature, several other macro abilities add even more power to the macro assembler. A good macro assembler should allow the user to pass information into a macro, as in the case of conditional jump macros.

The 8080 assembly language has no specialized set of jump or branch instructions for use after a compare. All its jump instructions are named after the condition flags they test. When doing a compare, you must be aware that the zero flag is set, if the two items were equal. Rather than remember what flag state corresponds to what logical state — no mean feat if you switch processors often — why not make up a new jump instruction for use after a compare? This instruction will jump, if the two values compared were equal.

To make a macro perform this function, you must pass into the macro the location you are supposed to jump to. It should come as no surprise that this is very easy to do. In defining the macro the programmer may specify a number of variables that will be passed into the body of the macro by the assembler. How do you do this? Consider the following:

```
;******************************
;* --> JEQ       where        *
;*   jump if equal to address where  *
;******************************

JEQ     MACRO   WHERE    ;create a macro, JEQ
        JZ      WHERE    ;pass location to jump
        ENDM             ;end the macro
```

In this example you are creating a macro called JEQ: jump if equal. In the macro definition you state that a single variable will be passed into the body of the macro by the use of the dummy variable WHERE. This means that, when you use the macro, any symbol placed in the WHERE position will be passed into the macro by the assembler. To use the macro, you enter:

```
use of macro                    assembler generates
        CPI     5                       CPI     5
        JEQ     SKIP   ------>           JZ      SKIP
        MVI     A,10                     MVI     A,10
SKIP:   RET                     SKIP:   RET
```

More than one variable may be passed into a macro. Suppose that one particular subroutine is used throughout a program to control lights. This subroutine needs to have two variables passed to it: the light to turn on, and the amount of time to keep it on. Typically you would write:

```
        MVI     A,5      ;turn on light 5
        MVI     C,20     ;for 20 seconds
        CALL    LIGHT    ;go do it
```

To perform the same function, a macro would need two variables passed to it. This macro might look as follows:

```
;*********************************
;*  --> FLASH     light, length        *
;*  flash light specified for length period  *
;*********************************

FLASH  MACRO  WHICH,LENGTH     ;pass in
       MVI    A,WHICH          ;which light to A
       MVI    C,LENGTH         ;time to C
       CALL   LIGHT            ;call routine
       ENDM                    ;end macro
```

When this macro is used, the program listing becomes much shorter and more readable. Each time the programmer wants to flash a light, only a single line of code needs to be typed. The following routine turns on light 1 for five seconds, followed by light 2 for 10 seconds:

```
;***************************************************
;*    ROUTINE TO TURN ON ONE LIGHT FOR FIVE      *
;*    SECONDS FOLLOWED BY ANOTHER FOR TEN        *
;*    SECONDS. FIRST LIGHT CAN BE SKIPPED        *
;*    IF ACCUM SET TO 0 BEFORE CALL.             *
;***************************************************

DOLGHT: CPI    0            ;are we enabled?
        JEQ    DOLG10       ;no- forget first light
        FLASH  1,5          ;flash light 1, 5 sec
DOLG10: FLASH  2,10         ;flash light 2, 10 sec
        RET
```

This routine is equivalent to writing the following assembly-language code:

```
DOLGHT: CPI    0            ;are we enabled?
        JZ     DOLG10       ;no- skip first light
        MVI    A,1          ;set light
        MVI    C,5          ;set time
        CALL   LIGHT
DOLG10: MVI    A,2          ;set second light
        MVI    C,10         ;set time
        CALL   LIGHT
        RET
```

Concatenating Text

Another important feature of a macro assembler is the ability to join pieces of text together. This is called concatenating text. In this process the assembler combines two words or symbols into one. A special character is used to tell the assembler when to concatenate text. In these examples we will use the "&" character.

Example: A&B - - - - > AB

Your first question about concatenating text might be, "What possible use does it have?" There are a number of important reasons for wanting this ability; let's start with a simple one. Suppose you need a macro that will rotate the accumulator either left or right, depending upon a letter passed to it. What you need is a macro that does the following:

```
LDA        VARIABLE       ;get a number
ROTATE     L              ;rotate once left
STA        VARIABLE       ;save variable times 2
```

If you can concatenate text and pass a variable into your macro, you should have no trouble making up a ROTATE command. The following example shows how to do just that.

```
; ************************************************
; *    - - >     ROTATE direction                *
; *    rotate the accumulator in the direction specified  *
; ************************************************

ROTATE  MACRO   DIRECT    ;macro, pass direction into it
        R&DIRECT&C        ;make up a RLC or RRC command
        ENDM              ;end the macro
```

This macro operates as follows. The command is evoked by the string ROTATE X, where X may be either an "L" or an "R." When the assembler encounters the symbol ROTATE, it looks through its internal tables and decides that this is a macro. It also notes that one variable is passed into the macro. The assembler takes the variable following the ROTATE and passes it into the macro. If the variable is an "L," the assembler replaces the macro instruction

"ROTATE L" with the definition of that macro. At this point the assembler has the characters "R&L&C" instead of "ROTATE L." The assembler now does the concatenation, yielding "RLC." From this point on the assembly proceeds normally, since RLC is a legal instruction for the 8080. If "R" is used instead of "L," the assembler will generate a "RRC" instruction. Any other letter or number will generate an illegal instruction which the assembler will flag as an error.

Repeat Directive

The next macro function to consider is slightly different from what has been previously covered. This is the macro repeat function. Suppose you need to fill a section of your program memory 15 bytes long with the value, 0AAH. The 8080 assembler has an instruction, (DB — save data byte), that will save byte values in a program as you specify them. You do have to type them all in by hand. Your listing might look like this:

```
DB      0AAH,0AAH,0AAH,0AAH,0AAH,0AAH,0AAH,0AAH
DB      0AAH,0AAH,0AAH,0AAH,0AAH,0AAH,0AAH,0AAH
DB      0AAH,0AAH,0AAH,0AAH,0AAH,0AAH,0AAH,0AAH
DB      0AAH,0AAH,0AAH,0AAH,0AAH,0AAH,0AAH
```

As you can see this clutters up the listing. Also, it is difficult to count how many bytes there are in those four statements. It would be very easy to make a mistake in typing all these lines. An easier way to do this involves the repeat macro.

```
              REPT Directive
       Local   Opcode   Operand
   optional:   REPT     expression
```

The macro repeat function gives an easy solution to such problems. The repeat function consists of a repeat definition including the number of times to repeat, the text to be repeated, and an end macro command. To repeat 15 bytes of 0AAH, you would use:

```
REPT     15              ;repeat the following statement(s)
DB       0AAH            ;15 times
ENDM                     ;end the repeat
```

This example would generate exactly the same object code as your previous one. This command is much easier to type and understand. It is also somewhat shorter than the original. Note that a REPEAT macro requires its own ENDM statement to terminate the macro.

A better use for the macro repeat function can be found in a true macro rotate instruction. When you write a program that rotates the accumulator, your only concerns should be which direction and how many times. If you use the concatenate text and repeat macro functions, it is easy to construct just such a macro.

```
; *******************************************
; --> ROTATE direction,count              *
; * Rotate the accumulator count number of    *
; * times in the direction specified          *
; *******************************************


ROTATE  MACRO       DIR,COUNT       ;macro definition
        REPT        COUNT           ; \ repeat all lines till ENDM
        R&DIR&C                     ;  *make RXC, count times
        ENDM                        ; / end this repeat
        ENDM                        ; end of macro
```

This ROTATE macro is much more useful than the first one created. To use this macro, you need to pass which direction to rotate the accumulator and how many times to do so. The macro will automatically generate the proper number and type of instructions. A macro definition always needs an end macro statement, as does a repeat macro statement also. That is why there are two "ENDM" statements in this macro. The following example illustrates how to use this macro:

```
        LDA         VARIABLE        ;get a number
        ROTATE      L,3             ;shift left three times
        ORA         C               ;or in a bit
        ROTATE      R,2             ;shift right twice
        STA         VARIABLE        ;save it away
        RET                         ;exit routine
```

This program generates the following code —

```
LDA      VARIABLE     ;get a number
RLC                   ; \
RLC                   ;   shift left three times
RLC                   ; /
ORA      C            ;or in a bit
RRC                   ; \
RRC                   ; / shift right twice
STA      VARIABLE     ;save it away
RET                   ;exit routine
```

As can be seen from the expanded program, the direction variable gives you the particular type of instruction ("RRC" or "RLC"), while the count variable simply repeats the instruction as many times as was specified.

Local Directive

Many times, when constructing a macro, you must provide a label within the macro to jump to. The problem with putting a label inside a macro is that every time you use that macro, the same label will be defined to the assembler. This will cause the assembler to generate an error, as the same symbol has been defined more than once. Most macro assemblers give you a way around this problem by allowing you to tell the assembler that a particular symbol exists only inside that macro.

LOCAL Directive

Label	Opcode	Operand
– – –	LOCAL	label1, label2,. . .

An example of a macro that needs a label internally is a "jump if greater than" instruction for the 8080, JGT. A normal program would look something like this:

```
           CPI      25        ;check to see if A>25
           JZ       AROUND    ;no- skip
           JNC      WHERE     ;yes- jump to where
AROUND:    CPI      5         ;next instruction
```

To perform a jump if greater than, requires two jump instructions. The first jump is needed to avoid doing the second instruction if the processor flags are set to zero. A macro that will do the same thing follows:

```
;***********************************
;* - - >  JGT     where            *
;* jump if greater than to address where   *
;***********************************
```

```
JGT    MACRO   WHERE      ;macro definition
       LOCAL   SKIP       ;state variable SKIP is local
       JZ      SKIP       ;jump if not greater than
       JNC     WHERE      ;jump if greater than
SKIP   EQU     $          ;make label at next address
       ENDM               ;end macro
```

The word LOCAL tells the assembler that the label SKIP has meaning only within the body of this macro. SKIP will not occur in the assembler symbol table. This allows the JGT macro to be used more than once in a program without an error.

Exit Macro Directive

The exit macro command, EXITM, provides a way to terminate macro code generation. Any time the EXITM opcode is seen inside a macro, the assembler will automatically skip all code between that EXITM and the first ENDM opcode it encounters. Thus the EXITM command is really only useful inside a conditional assembly statement.

	EXITM Directive	
Label	Opcode	Operand
optional:	EXITM	

One use for the EXITM macro feature is in building tables. When you build tables in assembly language, you typically need some type of special character at the end of the table, to inform the routine using those tables that it has reached the end of the table.

Suppose you are writing a text editor. You will need a table that pairs ASCII letters (typed commands) with corresponding routine addresses. In assembly language this table would look as follows:

```
COMTBL: DB     'C'              ;\ change command
        DW     CHANGE           ;/
        DB     'D'              ;\ delete command
        DW     DELETE           ;/
        DB     'K'              ;\ kill line command
        DW     KILL             ;/
        DB     'S'              ;\ substitute string
        DW     SUBSTI           ;/
        DB     0FFH             ; end of table indicator
```

A few quick comments about this table are needed. First, you can see that it is hard to read the alternating DB and DW statements. Being hard to read, it will probably encourage mistakes in typing. The second thing to notice is the end-of-table indicator. A 0FFH is used to mark the end of the table. Since 0FFH is not a legal ASCII character, this will probably be a good choice.

With the aid of a macro you can make this table more readable. This will lessen the chance of a typing error and make the program more understandable. You can also use the EXITM function to generate the end-of-table indicator. A macro is needed for this function. This is what it looks like:

```
;********************************************
;* --> COMAND  character,routine           *
;* build a table of character bytes followed by  *
;* a two byte routine address              *
;********************************************

COMAND MACRO   CHAR,ROUTINE          ;define command macro
       IF CHAR EQ 0FFH                ;if CHAR = end of table
       DB      0FFH                   ;generate table end
       EXITM                          ;and skip to first ENDM
       ENDIF                          ;end the if
       DB      CHAR                   ;otherwise, save character
       DW      ROUTINE                ;and routine address
       ENDM                           ;end the macro
```

Using this macro the old character table becomes:

```
COMTBL: COMAND  'C',CHANGE           ;change command
        COMAND  'D',DELETE           ;delete command
        COMAND  'K',KILL             ;kill a line
        COMAND  'S',SUBSTI           ;substitute string
        COMAND  0FFH                 ;indicate end of table
```

This table written with macros generates exactly the same object code as the first table written in assembly language. But this one is more readable, and the possibility of typing errors is reduced. Also, it is simple. If each table entry needed three or four parameters, an assembly-language program would be nearly impossible to follow. Using macros for tables gives you the ability to make your tables closer to English, which makes them easier to construct.

Indefinite Repeat Directive

The last macro directive covered here is closely related to the macro repeat command. This new instruction is called the indefinite repeat. It allows you to construct macros that generate a variable amount of code, depending upon the amount of parameters passed into them.

IRP Directive

Label	Opcode	Operand
optional:	IRP	dummy parameter,<list>

Suppose a macro is needed that takes whatever the HL register pair points at and saves it in a specified memory variable. The macro should be able to handle any number of variables. The following example uses the IRP function to do just that:

```
.*************************************
;
;* --> SAVE      variable            *
;* save what HL registers point at in variable  *
.*************************************
;

SAVE   MACRO   VARIABLES          ;define the macro
       IRP     Vl, <VARIABLES>    ;indefinite repeat, pass
       MOV     M,A                ;variable to Vl
       INX     H                  ;get byte, move pointer
       STA     Vl                 ;save is passed variable
       ENDM                       ;end indefinite repeat
       ENDM                       ;end the macro
```

When this macro is used, all variable names passed into it must be enclosed by "<" and ">" characters. Each parameter between these brackets is passed to the dummy variable, one at a time. In use, the macro would look like this:

```
LXI    H,TABLE                        ;get table pointer
SAVE   <MOTFLG,RUNFLG,QUITFG>         ;MOTFLG=(TABLE),
                                      ;RUNFLG=(TABLE+1),
                                      ;QUITFG=(TABLE+2)
LXI    H,TABL2                        ;new table pointer
SAVE   <VARIAB,LASTFG>                ;VARIAB=(TABL2),
                                      ;LASTFG=(TABL2+1)
```

For each item inside the angle brackets, the assembler will generate the three assembly-language statements: a move, an increment, and a store. The actual code generated would look as follows:

with macros		assembler generates	
LXI	H,TABLE	LXI	H,TABLE
SAVE	<MOTFLG,RUNFLG,QUITFG>	MOV	A,M
		INX	H
		STA	MOTFLG
		MOV	A,M
		INX	H
		STA	RUNFLG
		MOV	A,M
		INX	H
		STA	QUITFG
LXI	H,TABL2	LXI	H,TABL2
SAVE	<VARIAB,LASTFG>	MOV	A,M
		INX	H
		STA	VARIAB
		MOV	A,M
		INX	H
		STA	LASTFG

As you can see from this example, two small one-line macros have generated a large amount of repetitive assembly code.

Another use for the IRP command is in making tables. Suppose you need a table of X and Y coordinates that will be sent to a graphics display. If this display has a 180 by 180 matrix, it doesn't seem reasonable to save both X and Y for each point. You could save considerable memory space and eliminate numerous potential typing errors by pairing a single Y coordinate with numerous X positions. You would use a table structure that looks like this:

Y, X1, X2, . . . Xn, End Mark

This type of structure allows the software to fetch the Y position first (since it must be sent to the display each time), and then fetch matching X positions. The pair of numbers is sent to the display, and the next X position is fetched. If the X position is equal to an end mark, this process will be stopped. The following macro utilizes the IRP function to do this:

```
;*****************************************
;* --> CRTTBL    x position,yposition        *
;* build a table of y posit. with matching x posit.  *
;*****************************************
```

```
CRTTBL  MACRO   X,Y             ;define the CRT macro
        DB      Y               ;save y position first
        IRP     X1,<X>          ;pass all X to variable X1
        DB      X1              ;save the x position
        ENDM                    ;end indefinite repeat
        DB      0FFH            ;put end mark last
        ENDM                    ;end the macro
```

In use it looks as follows:

```
CRTTBL  <0,3,4>,1       ;all x for Y=1
CRTTBL  <7,9>,2         ;all x for Y=2
```

and generates the following code:

```
DB      1       ;Y position
DB      0       ; \
DB      3       ;  *X positions
DB      4       ; /
DB      0FFH    ;end Y=1 position
---------------------------------
DB      2       ;next Y position
DB      7       ; \
DB      9       ; / X positions
DB      0FFH    ;end Y=2 position
```

To summarize: an indefinite repeat takes a list of variables and assigns them, one at a time, to a dummy parameter. This dummy parameter is then passed into the macro for it to use. The process is repeated automatically until no more items exist in the list. The list is defined as all items between a pair of angle brackets.

USING MACROS

The previous section dealt with how to understand and construct macros. But the real question is, what can macros do for you? No one will use a special feature of an assembler just because it is there. There has to be some advantage to be gained by using it. So what can macros do for you?

The easiest way to answer this is to look at several macro examples. These macros were all developed for the 8080 microprocessor and are in constant use by numerous programmers. They have become popular because they make programming easier.

General Purpose 8080 Macros

```
;********************************************
;* --> DEC    register pair, number of times      *
;* decrement the register pair specified as many times  *
;* as instructed                                 *
;********************************************

DEC MACRO    REGIST,TIMES        ;macro definition
    REPT     TIMES               ;repeat next instruction
    DCX      REGIST              ;decrement indicated register
    ENDM                         ;end the repeat
    ENDM                         ;end the macro


;********************************************
;* --> IFA    condition,value,where               *
;* if the accumulator when compared to the value matches  *
;* the condition, jump to specified address       *
;********************************************

IFA MACRO    COND,VALUE,WHERE
    CPI      VALUE               ;check acc against value
    J&COND   WHERE               ;make jump instruction
    ENDM                         ;end the macro


;********************************************
;* --> INC    register pair, number of times      *
;* increment the register pair specified as many times  *
;* as instructed                                 *
;********************************************
```

```
INC        MACRO      REGIST,TIMES          ;macro definition
           REPT       TIMES                 ;repeat next instruction
           INX        REGIST                ;increment indicated register
           ENDM                             ;end the repeat
           ENDM                             ;end the macro


;**************************************
;* --> JEQ      where                    *
;* jump if after a compare the values were equal   *
;**************************************


JEQ        MACRO      WHERE                 ;macro definition
           JZ         WHERE                 ;equal means zero flag set
           ENDM                             ;end the definition


;**************************************
;* --> JFALSE    variable,where           *
;* jump if variable is false to address specified  *
;**************************************


JFALSE     MACRO      WHAT,WHERE            ;macro definition
           LOAD       WHAT                  ;use another macro inside
           JZ         WHERE                 ;false = 0
           ENDM                             ;end the macro


;****************************************
;* --> JGE      where                      *
;* jump if after a compare the accumulator was greater  *
;* than or equal to the number compared         *
;****************************************


JGE        MACRO      WHERE          '      ;macro definition
           JZ         WHERE                 ;if zero flag set or
           JNC        WHERE                 ;no carry then jump
           ENDM                             ;end the macro


;****************************************
;* --> JGT      where                      *
;* jump if after a compare the accumulator was greater  *
;* than the number compared                     *
;****************************************


JGT        MACRO      WHERE                 ;macro definition
           LOCAL      SKIP                  ;make a local label
           JZ         SKIP                  ;if zero flag set ignore
           JNC        WHERE                 ;on carry jump
```

```
SKIP      EQU      $                      ;jump around label
          ENDM                            ;end the macro


;**********************************************
;* --> JLE      where                        *
;* jump if after a compare the accumulator is less than  *
;* or equal to the number compared           *
;**********************************************


JLE       MACRO    WHERE                  ;macro definition
          JZ       WHERE                  ;jump if equal
          JC       WHERE                  ;jump if less than
          ENDM                            ;end macro


;**********************************************
;* --> JLT      where                        *
;* jump if after a compare the accumulator is less than  *
;* the number compared                       *
;**********************************************


JLT       MACRO    WHERE                  ;macro definition
          JC       WHERE                  ;jump if less than
          ENDM                            ;end the macro


;**********************************************
;* --> JNE      where                        *
;* jump if after a compare the values were not equal    *
;**********************************************


JNE       MACRO    WHERE                  ;macro definition
          JNZ      WHERE                  ;not equal means not zero
          ENDM                            ;end the definition


;**********************************************
;* --> JTRUE    variable,where                *
;* jump if variable is true to address specified   *
;**********************************************


JTRUE     MACRO    WHAT,WHERE             ;macro definition
          LOAD     WHAT                   ;use another macro inside
          JNZ      WHERE                  ;true = not 0
          ENDM                            ;end the macro
```

```
;***********************************************
;* - - >  LOAD   variable                      *
;* get variable into the accumulator and set processor  *
;* flags accordingly (8080 doesn't do this automatically)  *
;***********************************************

LOAD    MACRO   WHAT            ;define what to get
        LDA     WHAT            ;fetch byte to acc
        ORA     A               ;set flags with OR
        ENDM                    ;end this macro


;*****************************
;* - - >  POPALL                  *
;* restore all registers from the stack  *
;*****************************

POPALL  MACRO                   ;pop all registers
        POP     PSW             ;from the stack
        POP     B               ;in the same
        POP     D               ;order they were
        POP     H               ;put on it
        ENDM                    ;end this macro


;*************************
;* - - >  PSHALL               *
;* save all registers on the stack   *
;*************************

PSHALL  MACRO                   ;push all registers
        PUSH    H               ;onto the stack
        PUSH    D               ;in the same
        PUSH    B               ;order they will
        PUSH    PSW             ;be removed from it
        ENDM                    ;end this macro


;***********************************************
;* - - >  ROTATE   direction,times             *
;* rotate the accumulator in direction specified however  *
;* many times you were told                    *
;***********************************************

ROTATE  MACRO   DIR,TIMES       ;macro definition
        REPT    TIMES           ;repeat rotate
        R&DIR&C                 ;make rotate instruction
        ENDM                    ;end the repeat
        ENDM                    ;end the macro
```

```
;*************************************************
;* - - >  STORE   where,what                    *
;* save number at address specified, optimize for 0 case    *
;*************************************************
```

```
STORE     MACRO     WHERE,WHAT          ;macro definition
          IF WHAT   EQ 0                ;if variable = 0
          XRA       A                   ;use 1 byte acc=0
          ELSE                          ;otherwise
          MVI       A,WHAT              ;move immediate to acc
          ENDIF                         ;number what
          STA       WHERE               ;and save where told
          ENDM                          ;end the macro
```

```
;*************************************************
;* - - >  WHILE label,variable,condition,number    *
;* - - >  WEND   label                           *
;* as long as variable compares to the specified number    *
;* by the given condition repeat a loop defined by the      *
;* WHILE and WEND macros                         *
;*************************************************
```

```
WHILE     MACRO     X,VARIAB,COND,NUMBER
          LOCAL     SKIP                ;make internal label
WHIL&X    LDA       VARIAB              ;get the variable
          CPI       NUMBER              ;and compare to number
          J&COND    SKIP                ;do code if condition met
          JMP       WEND&X              ;otherwise quit
SKIP      EQU       $                   ;place to jump to
          ENDM                          ;end of macro
```

```
WEND      MACRO     X
          JMP       WHIL&X              ;jump back to while
WEND&X    EQU       $                   ;leave label to exit by
          ENDM                          ;end the definition
```

Macros in Use

Now that you have seen a library of macros, you should have a good
idea of their true power. Some macros help to eliminate the tedious
task of typing the same lines of code over and over. Examples of this
type of macro include the INC, DEC, LOAD, PSHALL, POPALL,
and ROTATE commands. Other macros can perform logical operations, as for instance the IFA and WHILE macros, which let you

perform high-level functions in assembly language without having to switch languages.

The use of this macro library will also make a program more readable. The macros are shorter than the matching assembly-language code and closer to English. This makes your program shorter and more understandable. Also, you don't have to worry as much about typing mistakes, since with macros you are typing less.

The following example shows the same program written in two different ways. The first section of code is written using macros wherever possible. The second piece is written in straight assembly language and is equivalent to the first program.

```
;************************************************
;*  The following routine must check first to see if it is      *
;*  running. If so it must exit. Otherwise it should enable     *
;*  an interrupt driven timer and toggle various output         *
;*  bits. This routine will need a new macro defined below.      *
;************************************************

;   - - >       OUTPUT    port,value
;   send value to output port specified

OUTPUT    MACRO     PORT,VALUE        ;macro definition
          MVI       A,VALUE           ;put value in acc
          OUT       PORT              ;and send out port
          ENDM                        ;macro end

MOTOR:    DI                          ;no interrupts for now
          JTRUE     MOTON,MOTEXT      ;if motor on, quit
          STORE     MOTON,TRUE        ;otherwise set flag
          STORE     TIME,50           ;set timer count
          EI                          ;restore interrupts
          WHILE     1,TIME,GT,25      ;as long as time
          OUTPUT    PORT85,1          ;is greater than 25
          OUTPUT    PORT85,2          ;toggle output bits
          WEND      1                 ;end this loop
          WHILE     2,TIME,GT,1       as long as time
          OUTPUT    PORT85,4          ;is greater than 1
          OUTPUT    PORT85,8          ;toggle different bits
          WEND      2                 ;end this loop
          OUTPUT    PORT85,0FFH       ;set all bits on
          STORE     MOTON,FALSE       ;turn off flag
MOTEXT:   EI                          ;interrupts back
          RET                         ;routine is done
```

;This routine can also be written as follows:

```
MOTOR:    DI                      ;interrupts off
          LDA      MOTON          ;get motor flag
          ORA      A              ;is it on
          JNZ      MOTEXT         ;yes- quit
          MVI      A,0FFH         ;otherwise
          STA      MOTON          ;turn it on
          MVI      A,50           ;also set up time
          STA      TIME
          EI                      ;enable interrupts
MOT10:    LDA      TIME           ;get time
          CPI      25             ;and check to see
          JC       MOT20          ;if out of range
          MVI      A,1            ;no- toggle bits
          OUT      PORT85
          MVI      A,2
          OUT      PORT85
          JMP      MOT10          ;repeat this loop
MOT20:    LDA      TIME           ;get time again
          CPI      1              ;is it in new range?
          JC       MOT30          ;no- jump
          MVI      A,4            ;yes-
          OUT      PORT85         ;toggle different bits
          MVI      A,8
          OUT      PORT85
          JMP      MOT20          ;go loop again
MOT30:    MVI      A,0FFH         ;set all bits on
          OUT      PORT85         ;at this port
          XRA      A              ;clear the motor flag
          STA      MOTON
MOTEXT:   EI                      ;enable interrupts
          RET                     ;end routine
```

The major differences between these two routines concern only length and readability. Assembly-language programs tend to be long and detailed. The more typing involved, the greater the chance for a typing error. The routine written with macros is much shorter and closer to English; it will be easier to write and debug.

INCLUDING FILES

The last feature of the advanced assembler to be discussed may not at first glance seem as useful. This feature is the ability to include separate disk files into the main body of a program. A good assembler lets you specify that the following piece of program is not actually here in this module; rather, it resides on the floppy disk under the name XXXXXX.YYY. This include-file feature can be a powerful programming tool.

This feature functions in much the same way as the macro command. A special statement is placed inside a program telling the assembler the name of the file to look for. When the assembler encounters the statement, it essentially replaces it with the text found in the disk file specified. A macro command tells the assembler to replace the macro call with the macro definition text.

A couple of examples of how to invoke an include file for various assemblers follow. They work with several different 8080 and Z80 assemblers.

```
$INCLUDE(:F1:FILE.EXT)
Where:
        $INCLUDE( ) is the assembler include command
        :F1: is the floppy disk drive the file is on (1)
        and FILE.EXT is the name of the disk file to include
INCLUDE A:NAME.EXT
Where:
        INCLUDE is the assembler include command
        A: is the floppy disk drive the file is on (A)
        and NAME.EXT is the name of the disk file to include
```

Now that you have seen a few examples of how this command can be invoked, you are probably asking yourself, what good is this instruction? What reason can there be for dividing program modules up into separate disk files? Actually, there are a number of very good reasons for using this particular command. The next section will discuss five of them.

Include-File Uses

Assume that you have an assembly-language program made up of several program modules. Each of these modules is going to need a copyright notice, a date, and a macro library. Since these three items are identical in each program module, it does not make sense to type each one individually. This sounds like a good use for the include-file feature. Another use for include files concerns tables. The source code for table entries can be placed into data files and included into the main module for assembly. The last use for include files is system-wide equates. If hardware or software variables need to be used by numerous program modules, it makes sense to group all these equates together in one file and let any program module that needs these definitions include this file.

Macro Libraries. A good portion of this chapter is devoted to macros. For all their numerous advantages, they do have one major drawback. If you are going to use a macro or group of macros, they must be defined. A big macro library is very useful, but an ordeal to type. If your program consists of more than one module, all macros must be defined in each individual module. Rather than type macro definitions into each program module, make one disk file called MACRO.LIB. This macro definition file will contain all common macros. Any program module that wants to use these macros need only use the include function to gain access to them.

This brings up a minor but useful assembler feature. Most assemblers allow you to control what assembly-language text is printed. Typically they have commands such as LIST and NOLIST. In the case of the macro definition file, you probably don't want to see the macro library listed in each program module. You can make one listing of it and keep that listing with the rest of your program modules. Thus the first statement inside your macro library will be NOLIST and the last statement will be LIST. This tells the assembler not to list the macro file in the main body of all your program modules.

By using the include-file command along with LIST and NOLIST instructions, you can create a general-purpose macro library for all your program modules. This library can also be copied from system to system, since it is not particular to any one program.

Date Files. Most assemblers allow some type of title line to be displayed at the beginning of each listing page. This is a useful feature and, when combined with the include command, gives you some interesting abilities.

By building a disk file that contains only a title command on your program disk, you have the ability to title and date each program that is assembled that day without reediting those programs. The disk file could be named TITLE.TXT. It would consist of a single line: a title command to your assembler. The title command might mention the system name and the current date as follows:

TITLE 'Motor Speed Control ** January 15, 1984 **'

Each program module would include that title file into itself. Thus if you make up a single title or date file per disk, all programs assembled on that disk will contain a common title and date.

The date is an important part of the title line, for it helps reduce confusion. Most computer areas become littered with old listing after a while. If each listing has a date on it, figuring out which is the latest listing is easy. The reason for using the include-file feature for the date is that it is easier to remember to change one common date file rather than all the programs to be assembled that day.

Copyrights.   More and more programs are carrying copyright notices these days. Since a proper copyright notice can take up an entire page, it would be a waste of time to type it into each individual program module. Even if your text editor allows you to merge files, so you need type the copyright file only once, you will still be wasting much disk space with multiple images of the same copyright notice.

The include-file feature of your assembler will do the same job with less effort. Make a file called CPYRIT.TXT to contain the complete copyright notice for your company. From then on, use the include feature to bring this file into each program module. This will place the same copyright notice on each listing without wasting either disk space or typing effort.

Data Files for Tables.   Quite often very complex assembly-language programs can be made much simpler by making use of tables. The tables can be constructed with macros, which will make them easy to understand and more readable. Sometimes, however, the program simplification comes with a price attached to it, since the tables can become exceedingly complicated. You might end up with five or six different tables that must be assembled together. Editing the table file can then become difficult.

A way around this problem is to use the include-file feature. Construct one program module that contains all the table macros and program definitions. Each individual table is in a separate disk file. The main program module simply includes these individual tables together into the main module, where they are assembled. The module might look like this:

```
INCLUDE A:CPYRIT.TXT

      NAME     TABLE

INCLUDE A:MACRO.LIB

      CSEG

INCLUDE A:TABLE1.DTA
INCLUDE B:TABLE2.DTA
INCLUDE A:TABLE3.DTA
INCLUDE A:TABLE4.DTA

      END
```

This type of format allows each table type to be individually entered. With very long or very complicated tables, this becomes an important advantage.

System-wide Equates.   A typical program will have several modules that all need to look at the same definitions. There might be common hardware ports, memory addresses, or special label values that several independent program modules need. If you define these values in each program module, you may run into a problem. When a port address changes, you must locate every program module that defined that address and change all these references. If you miss only one, your program is not going to work.

Another approach is to define all common equates in one disk file. Any program module that needs these values can include this file. When any change is needed, only this one file need be modified. Of course you still reassemble all the programs that use these values.

A better approach makes use of the relocatable assembler's PUBLIC and EXTRN commands. Instead of using an include file, build a program module that contains only system-wide equates. Each symbol is declared public. All program modules that need these values simply declare them external. When a port address changes, all you need to do is change that value in the system-equate module. Once this one module is reassembled, the link and locate process will fix all other references to this variable without needing to locate and reassemble any other modules.

There are five major uses for the include-file feature of an assembler. Four of these: macro libraries, date files, copyrights, and data files for tables, are helpful for everyday programming. The final use, system-wide equates, is best handled in another manner. In this case, it makes more sense to use the public and external assembler commands.

7
Assembler Techniques

PROGRAM ORGANIZATION

Programming in assembly language can be a difficult task. Therefore anything that makes your task easier should be welcomed with open arms. One sure way to simplify your program is to be consistent in its organization.

What is meant by consistent program organization, and how does this ease the programming burden? Consistent programming always puts the same piece or type of code in one particular place in your program. You follow the same order for all single programs or program modules. An example might be the equates section of a program: instead of having symbols equated to numbers throughout your program, why not put them all in one place? They could also be in alphabetical order, so each particular symbol will be easy to locate. As for location, it would be a good idea to place this group of equates near the front of the program module, so they will be easy to locate and change, if necessary.

Why go to all this trouble? Actually, it involves very little trouble, if any, and it is all for your own personal convenience. You are the one who will have to hunt through a program for the equate you need to change. Which is easier — an alphabetical list of equates at the beginning of a program, or a scattering of equates throughout the body of your listing? Since you are the one working on the program, make it easy on yourself: be consistent and organized.

The following sections describe one method for organizing your programs. This is not the only way to arrange assembly-language programs, but it is a consistent and easy method to follow. The essential is to be consistent in whatever organization you choose. You should be able to go back to a program you wrote three years ago and find that it is organized in much the same way as the program you are writing today.

Header Blocks

A header block should always be found at the beginning of a program. The purpose of the header block is to give each person looking at that program some minimal information about it. You should not have to leaf through a program to discover the most basic information about its function and history. A header block should provide this information at a glance.

The header block can usually be divided into three or four separate sections: the module descriptor block, a module history list, a pseudocode block, and — optionally — a module narrative. Each of these blocks or sections has its own special purpose. Examples of each of these types of header blocks can be found in Figures 7-1 through 7-5 respectively.

The Descriptor Block. This block is designed to provide minimal information about the program module. It should contain the program module name, version number, author, and date of last

```
;* ************************MODULE SPECIFICATION*************************
;*                                                                      *
;*    Name: COMERR                                                      *
;*                                                                      *
;*    Version: 1.20                                                     *
;*                                                                      *
;*    Date of last edit: 04/11/83                                       *
;*                                                                      *
;*    Author: G. ELFRING                                                *
;*                                                                      *
;* ------------------------------------------------------------------ *
;*                                                                      *
;*    Function: REPORT ALL ERRORS TO DISPLAY                            *
;*                                                                      *
;*    Inputs: NONE                                                      *
;*                                                                      *
;*    Outputs: SCREEN CONTROL PORT 84H                                  *
;*                                                                      *
;*    External Subroutines: HEXASC, ERRCHK                              *
;*                                                                      *
;*    Public Routines: COMERR                                           *
;*                                                                      *
;*    Run Mechanism: CALLED BY ANY PROGRAM                              *
;*                                                                      *
;*    Notes: ERROR CODE PASSED IN BC REGISTERS, MUST BE INITIALIZED BY  *
;*    CALLING COMINI.                                                   *
;*                                                                      *
;* ********************************************************************
```

Figure 7-1. A module descriptor block. The module descriptor block provides a quick specification for a program module. It should define what a module does at a single glance.

```
;* *************************MODULE SPECIFICATION****************************
;*                                                                         *
;*    NAME COMMER;                                                         *
;*                                                                         *
;*    Version: 1.20                                                        *
;*                                                                         *
;*    Date of last edit: 09/30/83                                          *
;*                                                                         *
;*    Author: G. ELFRING                                                   *
;*                                                                         *
;*    ------------------------------------------------------------------  *
;*                                                                         *
;*    Function: REPORT ALL ERRORS TO DISPLAY                               *
;*                                                                         *
;*    Inputs: NONE                                                         *
;*                                                                         *
;*    Outputs: SCREEN CONTROL PORT 84H                                     *
;*                                                                         *
;*    External Subroutines:                                                *
;*       EXTRN    HEXASC;     Convert hex to ASCII routine                 *
;*       EXTRN    ERRCHK;     Compare error code to standard errors        *
;*                                                                         *
;*    External Memory:                                                     *
;*       EXTRN    ERRCOD;     Error code stored here                       *
;*                                                                         *
;*    Public Routines:                                                     *
;*       PUBLIC   COMMER;     Main entry point for error routine           *
;*                                                                         *
;*    Public Memory:                                                       *
;*       PUBLIC   NEWERR;     Newest error saved here                      *
;*                                                                         *
;*    Run Mechanism: CALLED BY ANY PROGRAM                                 *
;*                                                                         *
;*    Notes: ERROR CODE PASSED IN BC REGISTERS, MUST BE INITIALIZED BY     *
;*    CALLING COMINI.                                                      *
;*                                                                         *
;* *************************************************************************
```

Figure 7-2. An alternative method of descriptor block construction. This block not only provides an English description, but also does the actual PUBLIC and EXTERN definitions for the relocatable assembler.

```
;* *************************** MODULE HISTORY ****************************
;*                                                                        *
;*    Date       Version          Description of Change                   *
;*    11/08/82   1.0       COUNT OVER RANGE FIXED, CNT NOW 2 BYTES         *
;*    12/03/82   1.1       ERROR LOOK UP TABLE MODIFIED FOR DEAD END STOP  *
;*                         FUNCTION                                        *
;*    12/05/82   1.1       TOP POWER FUSE GOOD CHECK ADDED TO MOVE         *
;*    12/08/83   1.2       TABLES CHANGED TO MACRO FORM                    *
;*    03/30/83   1.3       ERROR IN CONVERT MACRO FIXED, COULDN'T USE      *
;*                         CONVERSION FACTOR 0                             *
;*                                                                        *
;* **********************************************************************
```

Figure 7-3. The module history. The module history describes all changes that have been made to this module. It also provides a date and version number for each change. This information can be invaluable when debugging program modules.

```
;*********************** MODULE LOGIC DESCRIPTION ********************
;*                                                                  *
;*    Set up temporary magnet data base and customer list           *
;*    Print background screen                                       *
;*    Do forever                                                    *
;*        Blank screen variables                                    *
;*        Get a location label                                      *
;*        If location label is blank                                *
;*            Check and see if all single magnets should be added to the data base *
;*            Return to main menu                                   *
;*        Endif                                                     *
;*        Get reversible magnet information                         *
;*        If magnet is reversible                                   *
;*            Locate next single row, reversible, available magnet  *
;*        Else                                                      *
;*            Locate next single row, non-reversible                *
;*        Endif                                                     *
;*        Do while magnet code is not ok                            *
;*            If end of file reached                                *
;*                Say none found                                    *
;*            Else                                                  *
;*                Say magnet code                                   *
;*                Say magnet used                                   *
;*            Endif                                                 *
;*            Get magnet ok information                             *
;*            If not ok                                             *
;*                Set not used                                      *
;*                Searched for next record                          *
;*            Endif                                                 *
;*        Enddo while magnet is not ok                              *
;*        Update customer data base with current magnet and label information *
;*    Endodo forever                                                *
;*                                                                  *
;********************************************************************
```

Figure 7-4. The pseudocode block. The pseudocode block gives an English-language flow chart for your program. The description should be easy to understand. It forms the basis for the program code you write.

edit. It should also provide information about all hardware input and output performed by this module. Some description of how this module is run and what it controls should likewise be provided. Finally, a short description (two lines or less) of the function of this module and a small note area would be helpful.

The Module History. This header block is very important. It briefly describes every change made to this program module. It should also include the date the change was made, the program version number at the time, and, optionally, the person who made the change. This block should provide enough information at one glance to tell the history and present state of the module.

```
;**************************MODULE NARRATIVE****************************
;*                                                                    *
;*                                                                    *
;*  This procedure is called by GUIDANCE$AND$BLOCKING$PROC and by     *
;*  BLOCKING$TASK$AT$SYNC$TIME to output vehicle speed commands via the *
;*  Delayed Operations (DOP) subsystem.                               *
;*                                                                    *
;*  In order to achieve maximum material throughput in the system, delays are applied *
;*  only to commands that will slow the vehicle. We ignore the passed delay for any *
;*  command that increases the present speed and substitute a delay of IMMEDIATE. *
;*  (Note: this does not apply to the Clear Delay Pending Flag command which always *
;*  uses the passed delay.                                            *
;*                                                                    *
;*  Note that a hold command is not a change speed command such as SLOW. Instead, it *
;*  forces the vehicle to stop but does not change the hardware speed setting. If a hold is *
;*  sent to the vehicle it must be cleared when we resume motion. This is done by sending *
;*  a CLEAR$HOLD command before sending any speed change command (except hold *
;*  of course). The CLEAR$HOLD command is sent with the same priority and delay as *
;*  the speed change command so it will take effect at the same time. *
;*                                                                    *
;*  Since the trailer function handler must control speed while executing trailer operations *
;*  (i.e., Stop Operations) we must keep track of the last change speed command and not *
;*  send another of the same type. The LAST$SPEED is initialized when we receive an *
;*  INIT$SPEED command from NMR.                                      *
;*                                                                    *
;*  HOLD$DECISION sets the VEHICLE$SPEED to NO$HOLD$DECISION if the vehicle *
;*  is executing stop functions. In this case we must send the Clear Delay Pending Flag *
;*  command (if required) but no HOLD or speed change commands are performed. *
;*                                                                    *
;*  DOP handles all interfacing to the vehicle hardware and is capable of initiating *
;*  operations immediately or scheduling operations to occur after a predetermined delay *
;*  has expired. DOP also allows scheduling multiple operations or canceling previously *
;*  scheduled operations based on priority.                           *
;*                                                                    *
;**********************************************************************
```

Figure 7-5. The module narrative. The module narrative describes in English the operation of the module and the reasons behind this operation. This module provides reasons for the programming philosophy used in the module.

The Pseudocode Block. This section of the module header block describes the program flow in detail. Pseudocode is simply an English-language description of program logic. It is composed of IF and WHILE statements. The pseudocode block should be written before the program is coded and then be used to actually code the program. See Chapter 4 on "Structured Programming" for more details on pseudocode.

The Module Narrative. This block is an English-language narrative that describes not only what the program is doing but some of the reasons behind particular programming techniques. There are often several ways to write a program. The programmer will select one solution and implement it. There will rarely be any record of why that method was chosen, yet the reason might be significant. If you or another programmer decide to change that module at a later date, it would be helpful to know why the program was written the way it was.

Publics and Externals

The next items to consider in program organization are the public and external assembler directives. Usually there are not very many of these items, but they are important. When you link and locate a series of program modules for the first time, you may find that you have neglected to make certain symbols public. This being the case, you must search through your program modules to find where you neglected to make a proper definition. The list of public and external symbols should therefore be located near the beginning of the program, so you can quickly track down any errors in public or external definitions.

Equates

A well-written program should depend on equates rather than literal values for program control. If you must check numbers throughout a program against a maximum, it is to your advantage to define that maximum with an equate. Then, if the maximum changes, you need change only one equated value and reassemble the program. If you don't use equates, you must search through the entire program for all uses of that maximum value. If you miss any one of them, your program will have a serious error in it.

As mentioned previously, it is much easier to find and change an equate if it is located near the beginning of the program and not buried somewhere in it. Once all the equates are collected in one place, they should be arranged in alphabetical order to further simplify your job of locating one particular equate.

The Data Area

The next item to consider in program organization is the data storage area. Since a large number of programs written for microprocessors are designed to run under EPROM, always organize your modules as if your final program were to fit into that device. There is also another reason for having a separate data area: it is easier to find and change a memory variable, if all of them are located in one place.

Why not group all memory variables in each program module together? They could be arranged in alphabetical order and follow right behind the equate definition. This will allow any particular variable to be found and changed with ease. Since typically there are not a large number of memory variables in any given program, we will not have cluttered up the beginning of our program too much at this point.

Another reason for grouping all memory variables together has to do with the DSEG and CSEG commands. The assembler must be told that the following piece of program is to go into either RAM or EPROM, which requires the use of either the DSEG or CSEG assembler directives. The fewer times you must use these commands in a given program module, the less likely you are to forget one. Having one data area and one code area means that the DSEG and CSEG directives will each appear only once in a module, so you will not be likely to make a mistake with them.

The Code Area

It's about time we got to the main program code area. This, after all, is what writing programs is all about. All program code can follow the previously discussed items. It is usually a good idea to put the main routine of this program module first — once again, simply to make it easier to find. Similarly, utility subroutines should go near the end of this area.

The body of main program code can be fairly long even with program modules. It helps to organize your program, if you use page ejects to separate important pieces of a program module from one another. A program section that uses a table might be on the first few pages, followed by the actual table on a separate page.

Anything done to make this section of the program more readable will greatly help in the debugging stage. Large amounts of time will be spent debugging the code section of your program. An organized listing allows you to find errors more quickly. It also helps to organize your thoughts.

Initialization Area

The last section of code to be discussed is the initialization area of the program. Most program modules need some form of initialization before they can be run. This could mean setting several flags, initializing counters, or setting up pointers. Hardware devices might also have to be initialized.

It is a good idea to keep the initialization routines that are specific to one program module within that module. When a change occurs that requires a modification of the initialization routine, you stand a much better chance of making that change correctly if that code is located in the module it initializes. So where do you put the initialize routine? The only place left in the program listing that is easily accessible is the very end of the listing. If you put it there, you can always find it by simply turning to the last page of the listing.

Consistent program organization can be of great use to the assembly-language programmer. One way to organize assembly-language programs is to break them down into independent sections. These sections include header blocks, public and external definitions, equated variables, data areas, code areas, and initialization areas. See Figure 7-6 for a sample program organized in this manner. Consistently organizing all software modules in this way makes the programmer's job considerably easier. Good program organization can also make the software debugging task much easier.

INITIALIZING YOUR PROGRAMS

All assembly-language programs must have some type of initialization. Problems can arise in your programming when the initialization is done incorrectly. There are several techniques available for organizing the initialization process and controlling the initialization itself. These techniques can ensure that your software gets initialized properly. Using them will greatly decrease your debugging time. Programs are much easier to debug when all hardware is correctly set up and all software is properly initialized.

Each program module should have a single subroutine that is responsible for all initialization of both hardware and software in that module. In general, there should be very little hardware initialization in

```
;***********************************************************************
;*    Header and descriptor blocks go first                           *
;***********************************************************************
;
              NAME TEST                    ;modules should have a name

$INCLUDE(:F1:MACROF.SRC)                   ;all programs need macro library

              PUBLIC   START,STRINI,COUNT  ;public variable definitions

              EXTRN    CHECK,VARIAB        ;external variable definitions

FALSE         EQU      0                   ;\ module equates next
TRUE          EQU      0FFH                ;/

              DSEG                         ;data (RAM) area definitions

COUNT:        DS       1                   ;counter for routine
ONFLAG:       DS       1                   ;motor on when true

              CSEG                         ;following code goes into PROM

;***********************************************************************
;*    This space reserved for an explanation of main module           *
;***********************************************************************

START:        CALL     CHECK               ;main program module starts
              JZ       EXIT                ;first it proceeds on
              .                            ;until code is done
              .
              .
              STA      VARIAB              ;main routine comes to an end
              RET

;***********************************************************************
;*    This space reserved for an explanation of initialization        *
;***********************************************************************

STRINI:       MVI      A,4                 ;initialization routine goes
              .                            ;last
              .                            ;
              RET                          ;and ends with a return

              END                          ;this is the end of this module
```

Figure 7-6. A consistently organized program. A consistently organized program allows any section of it to be found with ease. Each portion of a program module will have its own individual space reserved for it.

the majority of program modules. This type of initialization belongs in the hardware control module. The program module initialization routines should take care of setting all RAM flags, counters, and pointers needed by that module. Upon program reset a single program should call each initialization subroutine in whatever order is needed to ensure an orderly system start-up.

```
;*****************************************************
;* THIS SECTION OF CODE MUST BE EXECUTED ON SYSTEM   *
;* POWER UP OR RESET.  NEW MODULE INITIALIZATION     *
;* ROUTINES SHOULD BE INCLUDED IN THIS LIST.  ORDER  *
;* OF ROUTINE INITIALIZATION IS IMPORTANT!           *
;*****************************************************

RESET:    CALL      INIPG1                  ;initialize module 1
          CALL      INIPG2                  ;initialize second module
          CALL      INIPG3                  ;initialize module 3
          CALL      INIPG4                  ;initialize fourth module
            .
            .
```

```
= = = = = = = = = = = = = = = = = = = = = = = = = = = = = = = = = = =
```

```
;*****************************************************
;* TYPICAL PROGRAM MODULE INITIALIZATION ROUTINE     *
;*****************************************************

          PUBLIC    INIPG1

          CSEG                              ;this program goes in PROM

INIPG1:   MVI       A,0FFH                  ;\ set up hardware
          OUT       PORT5E                  ;/ counter to accept
          MVI       A,LOW START             ;\ initial count
          OUT       PORT5F                  ;/ low byte. . .
          MVI       A,HIGH START            ;\ now high
          OUT       PORT5F                  ;/ byte. . .
          MVI       A,FALSE                 ;set motor on
          STA       MOTRON                  ;flag false
          STA       GOTKEY                  ;haven't got a key
          LXI       H,TABLE                 ;\ set up
          SHLD      POINTR                  ;/ pointer
          RET                               ;end of initialize routine
```

The only program modules that need to concern themselves with hardware are those one or two modules in charge of inputs and outputs for your system. Typically there will be only one main initialization module for hardware. This makes this area easier to find and correct, should hardware changes occur. Remember that hardware changes occur often in the early phases of product design. The hardware initialization subroutine should also be responsible for initializing all software that talks to this hardware. This includes all RAM variables, counters, and pointers needed by the module. This routine thus serves two functions: it sets up all hardware functions, and initializes the software used to control these functions.

There are several important things to consider when initializing RAM. Avoid trying to set all of memory to one particular state. This is a common technique used in many microprocessor systems, but it has a serious fault: it can mask errors in your program initialization. An error that is masked is simply an error that has not shown up yet; it can arise at any time.

If a program first zeros all memory, some memory variables may be either never initialized or initialized twice. The clearing of all memory may mask this fault. Only at a later date, when a variable must be initialized differently, will problems occur. The programmer may not be able to find the initialization routine for that variable, or there may be more that one routine that sets that variable. In this case the programmer may find only one of these routines. If he changes this one routine, there is still a problem somewhere else.

Setting all RAM at the beginning of a program is in effect admitting that you are not going to initialize program memory properly. You are saying that you don't know what routines use what variables, so you will fix them all at once. This is a poor solution to a simple problem. Every variable that needs to be initialized should be set in the routine that defines and uses that variable.

For RAM initialization it is a very good idea to individually set each flag, counter, or pointer to its proper state. This takes more code than simply clearing all of program memory, but it ensures that each variable is set correctly. It also enables you to find and change that variable's initialization at a later date, if the demand arises. Flags should be set to either true or false, as described later in this chapter. Counters should be set to their starting count, and pointers should be set to their starting value. By following this procedure you will be better able to understand and modify your program. The following initialization routine uses macros to improve its clarity.

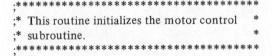

```
;*************************************
;* This routine initializes the motor control   *
;* subroutine.                                   *
;*************************************
```

```
MOTINI:   STORE     MOTFLG,FALSE        ;set motor off
          STORE     COUNTR,0            ;set count to 0
          STORE     DATFLG,TRUE         ;data processing allowed
          LXI       H,DATBUF            ;\ set up
          SHLD      POINTR              ;/ pointer
          RET                           ;end initialization
```

Multiple program modules can cause initialization problems. If two or more routines use the same flag or other variable, the question arises, which module defined and initialized this variable? We don't want two different modules trying to initialize the same variable, which can make bugs hard to find. One technique for avoiding this problem is to gather all RAM variables used by more than one program module into a single common module. This module could be called the public RAM module, PUBRAM. All its memory definitions and initializations are for public or common RAM. The purpose of this module is to ensure that there is only one place where any commonly used RAM is defined or initialized. This avoids errors and reduces confusion. Now, when looking for a common variable, a programmer need examine only one common module. The following example shows a complete public RAM module for a small system.

```
          NAME      PUBRAM              ;this is public ram module

          PUBLIC    MOTFLG, DATFLG, POINTR, DATBUF

          DSEG                          ;RAM definitions first

DATBUF:   DS        128                 ;data buffer, 128 characters
DATFLG:   DS        1                   ;true when data allowed
MOTFLG:   DS        1                   ;motor flag, true if on
POINTR:   DS        2                   ;pointer to data area

          CSEG

PUBINI:   STORE     MOTFLG,FALSE        ;set motor flag off
          STORE     DATFLG,TRUE         ;data is allowed
          LXI       H,DATBUF            ;\ set up
          SHLD      POINTR              ;/ pointer
          RET                           ;end the initialization

          END
```

TRUE AND FALSE FLAGS

Assembly-language programs often use flags to control program operation. Flags can be used to enable or disable certain operations, or to pass information between modules. The actual operation that most of these flags perform is to indicate one of two possible states. A flag typically indicates that something is true or false.

In minicomputers and mainframes, TRUE and FALSE are commonly used to indicate the state of a flag. This technique is easy to apply to assembly-language programming with microprocessors. All that needs to be done is to define the symbols TRUE and FALSE. Then programs can test to see whether a flag is true or false.

Minicomputers and mainframes have long had standard definitions for the true and false symbols. True has been defined as all bits being set or on. Thus true can be either 0FFH or 0FFFFH depending upon whether you are working with bytes or words. False has been defined as being the opposite of true or 0H.

Since these definitions of true and false already exist, it would be a good idea to follow them in your assembly-language programming. This will help you if you ever need to interface your programs to a higher level language (see Chapter 9). The equate feature of your assembler can be used to define the symbols true and false. A good place to put these equates would be in the macro library. Thus every program module that reads in the macro library will automatically have true and false defined for it.

The macro library can also include several special macros that take advantage of the true and false definitions. New instructions can be made that jump if a variable is true or false. These two new instructions can greatly improve the readability of a program. The following examples show how to construct and use jump-if-true and jump-if-false macros.

```
;********************************
;* Jump if flag is true of false macros    *
;********************************

FALSE     EQU     0               ; \ true and false
TRUE      EQU     0FFH            ; / definitions

JFALSE    MACRO   FLAG,WHERE      ;jump if flag false
          LDA     FLAG            ;get flag into accum
```

```
            ORA     A              ;set processor flags
            JZ      WHERE          ;jump if false
            ENDM                   ;end macro

JTRUE       MACRO   FLAG,WHERE     ;jump if flag true
            LDA     FLAG           ;get the flag
            ORA     A              ;set processor flags
            JNZ     WHERE          ;jump if true
            ENDM                   ;end the macro
```

In operation both these macros function in much the same way. Each macro requires a flag name and an address to jump to if the condition is met. The actual condition to jump on is selected by the name of the macro used. The two instructions, JTRUE and JFALSE, are easy to recognize and understand. An example of their use in programming follows.

```
;****************************************
;* This routine controls motor operation.  If the *
;* motor is already on − return.  Otherwise turn *
;* it on and check for an error.              *
;****************************************

MOTOR:   JTRUE    ONFLG,MOTEX      ;jump if motor on
         CALL     TURNON           ;turn on motor
         JTRUE    ONOKFG,MOTEX     ;jump if no error
         LXI      B,ERRMSG         ;load motor error message
         CALL     ERROR            ;and then report it
MOTEX:   RET                       ;common exit point
```

These commands are easy to read and understand. Each macro instruction occupies only a single line. This shorter format makes your program look more organized. The macros are also much closer to English. It is much harder to make a mistake while testing the state of a variable when using them. The function of a JTRUE instruction is obvious. Compare the JTRUE command to the JNZ instruction that it replaces. You will have a much harder time making a mistake with the JTRUE command than with the JNZ command. The less mistakes you make, the easier it will be to debug your program.

Some programmers do not like to use true and false flags because, in their opinion, using a whole byte of memory to save a yes or no state is a waste of memory. Well, it *is* a waste of memory. Memory has become very inexpensive of late, while at the same time programming has become more and more expensive. Any attempt to use more than two logical states per flag will complicate your program. This additional complication will usually cost more in design, coding, debugging, and maintenance time than could ever be saved by conserving a few bytes of memory. In an age where a 4K by 8 RAM chip can be purchased for from three to five dollars, one byte of memory is worth only 0.12 cents. By using simple true and false variables the programmer wastes a small amount of memory but gains a program that is simpler and easier to understand.

The purpose of true and false flags is to make your programs more readable and understandable. A program that reads a little closer to English will be that much easier to understand and debug. By keeping variable states to a maximum of two, your program will be kept logically simple. This makes the program easier to design and less likely to have serious bugs. Furthermore, program maintenance will be that much easier. Using the true and false jump macros will also shorten your program and speed up assembly time.

ONE EXIT FROM A SUBROUTINE

Assembly-language programming puts no restrictions on how a programmer chooses to exit from a routine. Most microprocessors allow some form of conditional return to be used. This makes it easy to construct routines that have numerous conditional exits. However, this multiplicity of exit points from a single routine will cause problems when debugging that routine or trying to make changes to it.

A more structured approach to assembly-language programming, as detailed in Chapter 4, allows only a single exit point from any subroutine or major program module. While it is probably not possible to write totally structured programs in assembly language, the idea of having only a single exit point from any routine is easy to follow. This implies that conditional returns should rarely, if ever, be used. Conditional returns in your program should be replaced by jump or branch instructions to a common exit point.

Why use a single-exit point from a routine? This technique is sure to waste memory space and may take longer to execute. The reason is there are several problems associated with multiple-exit points from a routine. It is difficult to follow the logic of a routine that has numerous exit points scattered throughout. It is difficult to debug a routine with more than one exit point. When testing it, you must identify each exit and set a breakpoint there. If one exit is missed, your test of the module may fail.

But the most important reason for avoiding multiple-exit points has to do with changing or modifying your program. A subroutine is often required to pass information back to the routine that called it. If a routine has multiple-exit points, this information must be set up before each point of return. If the program suddenly changes, thus changing the information that must be passed back, it is easier to make a change to the single-exit-point routine. If a routine has multiple exits, it is possible to overlook one exit point when making a change and thus introduce a subtle bug that occurs only under certain specific return conditions. A similar problem arises if your routine did not pass any information back to its caller but is now required to. It is much easier to change the single-exit-point routine than the multiple one.

The easiest way to avoid these problems is to make sure that all your routines have only a single exit point. All conditional return instructions should be replaced with conditional jumps to a common exit point. If at some later date you wish to pass a value back to the calling routine in the accumulator, this need be done only at the common exit point. Since all exits are done at this point, this routine is easy to modify. This type of programming operates in a straight-line sequence and ends in one specific spot.

The following example shows a subroutine with a common exit point. When written with macros, this routine becomes:

```
CKUPER:  MOV    A,C              ;get the character
         MVI    B,BAD            ;set bad
         IFA    LT,' ',EXIT      ;if < space- bad
         JEQ    GDEXIT           ;if space- good
         IFA    LT,'0',EXIT      ;if < '0'- bad
         IFA    GT,'9',EXIT      ;if > '9'- bad
GDEXIT:  MVI    B,GOOD           ;otherwise good
EXIT:    RET                     ;common exit
```

AVOID UNNECESSARY JUMPS

One of the major tenets of structured programming is the elimination of the jump instruction. While it might be possible to write an assembly-language program with no jumps in it, this is rarely if ever done. Jump or branch instructions are used to test conditions throughout most assembly-language programs. While most such programs need jump instructions, they do not need extra ones. Programs can be coded in many different ways, some of which use more jump instructions than others. Generally, the method that uses the fewest jump instructions is the best.

When programming, then, it is a good idea to use as few jump instructions as possible. Avoiding jumps makes your program more readable and easier to follow. It also makes a program logically simpler. Programming most assembly routines in-line usually results in a better program. Instead of testing for a condition and then jumping to another routine when that condition is met, test for the opposite condition. If it is not met, then do the required function. If it is met, then jump around the code performing the required function. This programming technique uses at least one less jump instruction than the jump-to-another-routine method, and is easier to read and follow as long as the functions being performed are not long. The following example shows the use of this programming technique:

```
            MVI     B,NOLINE        ;say no line yet
            CPI     CR              ;got return?
            JEQ     CHK10           ;yes- go say so
            CPI     LF              ;got line feed?
            JNE     CHK20           ;no- quit
CHK10:      MVI     B,LINE          ;set end of line
CHK20:      NOP                     ;program goes on. . .
              .
              .
              .
```

AVOID DEEPLY NESTED SUBROUTINES

One method of structuring assembly-language programming involves the use of subroutines. Subroutines can be used to perform the same functions that procedures are used for in high-level languages. While the use of subroutines can help structure your assembly-language programming, their use can become excessive.

Problems can arise when subroutines are nested too deeply. When one routine calls another that calls yet another, and so forth, these routines are said to be deeply nested. Deeply nested subroutines can result in programs that are very difficult to debug and maintain. During the debugging it often becomes necessary to trace program operation. A program containing deeply nested subroutines can be very difficult to trace through.

Suppose your program has a bug that seems to be associated with the operation of subroutine 1. You start debugging the program with breakpoints in that subroutine. If subroutine 1 calls another, you must locate the next subroutine in your program listing and then set breakpoints in it. But suppose this new subroutine calls yet another. This tracing process will go on until the last level of subroutines is reached. If you get to the last level and still haven't found the bug, you have to go back up the nested subroutines — not as easy task. Since your listing don't indicate which subroutines called which, the programmer will have to remember this. It thus becomes very difficult to return to the main line of your program.

It is a good idea, then, to avoid nesting subroutines more than three or four levels deep. This ensures that your assembly-language programs will be understandable and easy to follow. Subroutines can be used to structure your programs, but they should not be used excessively.

USING TABLE STRUCTURES

Making logical decisions in an assembly-language program can become quite difficult and tedious. Most decisions are accomplished through jump or branch instructions. Large numbers of jump instructions in a program make that software hard to read and difficult to follow. But another technique can be used that doesn't have these drawbacks: tables. Tables can greatly simplify a program, allowing it to run faster and shortening the amount of code needed to perform large numbers of decisions. There are two basic types: those used to make logical decisions, and those containing data or information. By using both, assembly-language programs can be simplified and improved.

Tables are often used to assist in making logical decisions. These tables can replace in-line program code that consists of large numbers of jump instructions. This type of table typically is used to replace five or more branch instructions. Consider a program that must compare a single byte to many different values. It will typically be written as a series of IF statements. In assembly language this will be done with pairs of compare and jump instructions. As the number of values to compare grows, so does the program length, execution time, and complexity. The large number of jump instructions used will make it difficult to follow the program.

A better way to write this program involves a table. The table would be organized as a series of entries, each with two values. The first value would be compared to the input value, while the second would be the address of the routine to jump to if the value matched the input. A small routine must be written that will search the table and perform the comparisons.

```
TABLE:   DB      0DH           ; \
         DW      CARRIA        ; / on CR go to routine
         DB      0AH           ; \
         DW      LINEFD        ; / on LF go to routine
         DB      09H           ; \
         DW      TAB           ; / on tab go to routine
         DB      0CH           ; \
         DW      FORMFD        ; / on form feed, go
         DB      0FFH          ;mark end of table
```

Suppose a text editor program has to be designed. One typical function of this type of program is to match an input character to a particular routine to handle that function. An input character of "K" might be interpreted as a kill-a-line command. Similarly "S" might mean substitute, and "D," delete a character. A command table could be used to match input characters to their appropriate handling routines.

The following program searches through a table to find a match to a character input to it. If this character is found in the table, the search routine will jump to a routine specified by the table to perform some function. That routine ends with a return instruction to bring program control back to the main line. Note the use of macros to generate the table.

```
EDIT       MACRO     CHAR,ROUTINE          ;this macro used to
           DB        CHAR                  ;generate table in
           DW        ROUTINE               ;proper order
           ENDM                            ;end of macro

TABLE:     EDIT      'K',KILL              ;kill a line
           EDIT      'S',SUBSTI            ;substitute
           EDIT      'D',DELETE            ;delete some characters
           EDIT      'L',LINES             ;move up/down lines
           DB        0FFH                  ;table end marker
```

```
;**********************************************************
;*  SEARCH A TABLE FOR A MATCH TO THE CHARACTER IN C  *
;**********************************************************
```

```
SEARCH:    LXI       H,ENDSRC              ;set up return address
           PUSH      H                     ;on stack
           LXI       H,TABLE               ;set pointer to table
SRCH10:    MOV       A,M                   ;get table character
           INX       H                     ;move pointer to address
           CPI       0FFH                  ;is this end of table?
           JEQ       ERROR                 ;yes- go do error
           CMP       C                     ;character match?
           JEQ       SRCH20                ;yes- go find address
           INX       H                     ; \ no-
           INX       H                     ; / move to next table entry
           JMP       SRCH10                ;go look again

SRCH20:    MOV       E,M                   ;found match so,
           INX       H                     ;get address of
           MOV       D,M                   ;routine into DE
           XCHG                            ;then put into HL
           PCHL                            ;and jump to it

ENDSRC:    NOP                             ;return here after routine
           •
           •
```

Data tables usually provide information to a program rather than helping it make decisions. Data tables can be used to translate one type or form of information into another. One example of this is commonly used in many programs. Suppose a binary number from zero to seven needs to be translated into its bit equivalent. The programmer needs a routine to turn zero into one, one into two, two into four, three into eight, and so forth. A table of all eight bit equivalent numbers could be made. A very short subroutine can now be constructed to use an input from zero to seven as an index into this table. Thus this table and routine can translate one form of number into another, as seen in the following example.

```
;***********************************************
;* TRANSLATE NUMBER 0-7 INTO BIT 0-7        *
;* INPUT NUMBER IN A, RETURN RESULT IN A    *
;***********************************************

XLATE:   LXI   H,BINARY      ;point to table
         ANI   7H            ;make sure only 3 bits
         MOV   E,A           ;put index into
         MVI   D,0           ;DE register pair
         DAD   D             ;add index to pointer
         MOV   A,M           ;get binary number
         RET                 ;return

BINARY:  DB    1             ;table of ascending bits
         DB    2
         DB    4
         DB    8
         DB    10H
         DB    20H
         DB    40H
         DB    80H
```

Data tables can frequently be variable in length. The variable-length format is used to conserve memory. This implies that these tables will be very big, since saving small amounts of memory is usually not worthwhile. The easiest way to make a variable-length table is through the use of macros. Macros help organize the table structure and facilitate the input of variable length entries.

Tables are often used to send information to a color graphics CRT. In this example we have a large number of points that we wish to display on a CRT. Rather than duplicate both X and Y coordinates each time we define a point on the screen, we can save storage space in our computer by having only one Y coordinate saved away for each of the multiple X coordinates. The table would have a Y coordinate followed by a variable number of X coordinates. The last byte of each entry must indicate that this is the end of this variable-length item. A macro that will generate this table follows:

```
                    Structure
                    Y
                    X1
                    X2
                    X3
                    •
                    •
                    Xn
                    ENDER

CRT     MACRO   X,Y                     ;X-Y table macro
        DB      Y                       ;save Y first
        IRP     X1, <X>                 ; \
        DB      X1                      ;  *save away all X
        ENDM                            ; /
        DB      0FFH                    ;end of entry
        ENDM                            ;end macro definition

TABLE:  CRT     <1,5,7,9,23> ,1              ;Y = 1
        CRT     <2,5,7,9,22,34> ,2           ;Y = 2
        CRT     <1,5,9> ,3                   ;Y = 3
        CRT     <3,5,6,11,17,19,21,33> ,4    ;Y = 4
        •
        •
        •
        DB      0FFH                                  ;end of table
```

This macro lets us generate complicated X-Y coordinate tables with only a single line entry for each Y coordinate. This type of table is very easy to enter and read. It is also easy to debug, since entries for each Y coordinate are all on a single line.

A more complicated type of table structure for saving information is called the linked list. Linked lists are typically used to organize information stored in RAM. Each piece of information is chained or linked to the next piece of information through the use of a pointer.

Linked lists can be best understood through an example. Suppose we have a UART which is receiving information from another computer. This UART will gather information until it sees a carriage return. It will then pass this information on to another program module to be processed. The actual UART handling routine is running under interrupt control. It is thus running in the background and is transparent to the user. This type of assembly-language programming is very easy to do and understand. However, problems can arise if information arrives at the UART faster than the processing routine can handle. If complete messages come in too quickly they will be lost, unless some method is devised to save them.

One technique for saving this information involves the use of duel data areas. The UART handling routine simply puts all its information into the first data area and then passes it to a routine which will process that information. The UART routine then switches to a second data area and proceeds to fill that up. Yet this type of routine can still run out of room to store the information, if the processing routine becomes overloaded or the computer is busy servicing other programs.

A better technique involves the use of a linked list. In this case the interrupt routine is allocated a fixed area of memory to put a message into. As characters come in, the interrupt routine places these characters into this memory area. When the message is complete, the interrupt routine passes this complete message area over to the next program module. The passing is accomplished by chaining or linking this RAM area to the previous pieces or messages that are on this list. The interrupt routine then asks for another fixed-memory area and places the next message into it. This process can repeat itself any number of times. Figure 7-7 shows how a linked list is put together and how data is stored in it.

As you can see from this figure, linked lists have some special features embedded in them. The first two bytes of the RAM area in a linked list are dedicated to a pointer to the next item on this chain. Thus each item is chained to the one after it. The last item in the chain has a pointer of 0FFFFH to identify it as the end item on this queue or list. Two other pointers are also used with this list that make up something called the anchor. The first pointer in the anchor points to the beginning item on the list, while the second points to the last item on the list. These two pointers make it easy to identify the beginning and end items on this list. The beginning item may be easily removed or popped from the queue, and new items may be entered at the end of the queue.

Linked lists are typically used to order data in a FIFO manner — first in, first out. Thus in our previous example, information from the UART will be queued in a FIFO manner on this list. The module which processes this information will remove items from the top or start of the queue, while the UART places new information on the

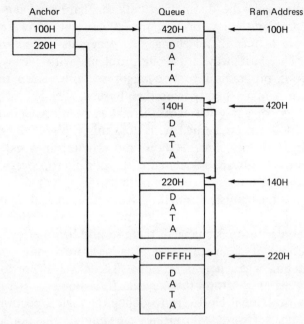

(0FFFFH is end of queue identifier)

Figure 7-7. A linked list of queue. A linked list or queue consists of a number of data areas chained together. The first two bytes of each data area are used to point to the next item on the chain. A special four-byte pointer called the anchor is also used. It contains a pointer to the beginning and to the end of the queue.

bottom or end of the queue. This ensures that the information will be processed in the same order that it came in.

Linked lists are typically used to process information from UARTs or other sources in a FIFO manner. They are also used a great deal in real-time executives (see Chapter 8).

SEPARATE THE LOGICAL FROM THE PHYSICAL

Microprocessors seem to blur the distinction between hardware and software. Many things that could be done in hardware are done with software in these systems. Microprocessors often seem to change the very environment they work in. What is done with software one day might be changed to hardware the next. The hardware itself may often change. Input states can change with each minor revision to hardware.

This blurring of the distinction between hardware and software can cause problems for your programs. Whenever hardware changes, you will have to locate and change any programs that reference that hardware. The best way to avoid problems with hardware is to separate your programs into two major sections. Keep the logical part of the program separate from the physical. The logical part does the calculation or analytical work; it makes decisions about what to do next, but is not concerned with how things physically get done. The physical section controls how and when things get done. It works with the hardware associated with your microprocessor system and may monitor inputs or control outputs.

Separating the physical portion from the logical makes your programming task easier because you minimize interactions between them. When hardware is changed, there should be no effect upon the logical section of your program. Furthermore, your program is easier to debug when it is in sections. The physical portion can be debugged separately from the logical. It is not necessary to have completely functional hardware to debug the logical portion of your software, since software test routines can simulate this portion of the program. The physical portion can be debugged in a similar manner and can be used to debug the actual hardware.

To separate the logical and physical sides of your program, make separate program modules to handle each function. The physical side of the program can usually be divided into two modules, one to control outputs and the other to monitor inputs. Logical programs that need to examine an input bit, as for instance a switch closure, will call subroutines resident in the physical input module. These routines will return a true or false value based on whether or not the switch was closed. This ensures that when hardware changes, the logical portion of the program will not be effected. Another advantage of this technique is that when a hardware change occurs, there is only one program module to modify. This module is easily found and the change is thus easy to implement. No other module is allowed to look at that input port. A further advantage results from turning all inputs into positive logic functions: these input routines all return true when a switch is closed, regardless of whether the actual bit is a zero or one when closed. Positive logic is much easier to debug and understand.

Inputs

```
;********************************************************
;* SWITCH DETECT ROUTINES, RETURN SWITCH STATUS AS    *
;* TRUE IF CLOSED, FALSE IF OPEN                      *
;********************************************************

SWITCH:  IN      PORTA8      ;read port
         ANI     2           ;check for right switch
         JZ      SCHEXT      ;if 0, accum is ok
         ORI     0FFH        ;set true
SCHEXT:  RET                 ;common exit

CHECK:   IN      PORTA8      ;read port
         CMA                 ;this switch low true
         ANI     80H         ;check this one only
         JZ      CHCK10      ;skip if not there
         ORI     0FFH        ;otherwise set true
CHCK10:  RET                 ;common exit
```

Outputs

```
;****************************************************
;* TURN ON OR OFF A LIGHT.  ON ENTRY A = LIGHT    *
;****************************************************

LITEON:  CALL    XLATE       ;translate light # to bit
         MOV     C,A         ;put light bit in C
         IN      PORT30      ;read port
         ORA     C           ;and or in light
         OUT     PORT30      ;send out lights
         RET                 ;end the return

LITEOF:  CALL    XLATE       ;translate light to bit
         CMA                 ;make up and mask
         MOV     C,A         ;and place in C
         IN      PORT30      ;read the lights
         ANA     C           ;mask out this light
         OUT     PORT30      ;and do it
         RET                 ;end routine
```

Program separation into logical and physical portions gives you a number of programming advantages. Program modules become more independent and more easily tested. Changes to hardware affect only one program module and are easy to implement. The program as a whole becomes easier to document and maintain owing to this modular programming approach. Finally, the hardware-dependent modules can be tested and debugged as soon as hardware is available. This helps ensure that the hardware is well debugged before the really serious software debugging starts.

SPECIAL PROGRAMMING TECHNIQUES

There are several specialized programming techniques that are mainly of use in assembly language. The ease of implementation of these techniques depends upon the individual architecture of the micro-processor you are using. The following sections describe some common techniques and give examples of their use.

Exclusive Or

The exclusive-or function is offered on almost all microprocessors. This particular instruction often causes more problems than it solves for one cannot easily visualize what it is doing. This instruction works in negative logic, indicating whether two particular bits are *not* the same. Because it produces a negative answer and operates bit-wise on an entire byte, the result of this instruction is often very difficult to understand. Avoid using this instruction if at all possible. The only major use for it occurs on processors that have no clear-the-accumulator command. The exclusive-or function is then often used to clear the accumulator.

Passing Information to a Subroutine

It is often necessary to call a subroutine and pass information to it. The programmer may also wish not to pass this information through the microprocessor registers. One easy technique for passing information to a subroutine involves manipulation of the machine's stack. In this case the subroutine call will be followed by the necessary information preserved in program memory (EPROM). On entry to the subroutine, the return address on the stack is actually pointing to this information. The subroutine can remove and use this pointer, and so has access to the passed information. The subroutine must then ensure that the pointer is moved past the data and placed back on the stack. Once this is done, the subroutine can execute a return instruction. Through this technique, information can be passed to a subroutine without having to be put into registers, as shown in the following example.

```
      Subroutine Call
          MVI    A,5          ; \ set up counter
          STA    COUNT        ; /
          CALL   EXAMIN       ;subroutine call!!
          DW     DATBUF       ;pass buffer pointer
          DB     CNTR         ;pass data count
          NOP                 ;return here


;*******************************************************
;*  THIS SUBROUTINE USES DATA PASSED IN THE THREE     *
;*  LOCATIONS FOLLOWING THE SUBROUTINE CALL           *
;*******************************************************

EXAMIN: POP    H            ;get the return address
        MOV    E,M          ;use it to fetch data
        INX    H            ;into the processor
        MOV    D,M          ;registers
        INX    H            ;point to counter
        MOV    C,M          ;byte and get it
        INX    H            ;point to real return
        PUSH   H            ;address and put back
          .
          .
          .
        RET                 ;routine exits normally
```

Conditional Subroutine Calls

Most microprocessors offer conditional call instructions. This type of command can be very useful, provided the programmer is careful about the way the subroutine is constructed. Suppose a program needs to examine a single byte and call each of eight possible subroutines, depending upon whether the appropriate bit is set in that byte. One way to do this is through the use of conditional call statements. The byte to be tested can be loaded into the accumulator. It is then rotated right, to put the least significant bit into the carry. A conditional call can be made to the proper subroutine, based on whether or not the carry is set. It is very important that the subroutine being called preserve the accumulator at its start and restore it before its end. This ensures that the next rotate and conditional call will work correctly. The following example shows how to implement this technique.

```
;****************************************
;*  Test for each bit in a byte.  Call routines     *
;*  based on bits set.                              *
;****************************************

            LDA     TSTBIT          ;get byte to test
            RRC                     ;is bit 0 on?
            CC      CONV01          ;yes- call CONV01
            RRC                     ;is bit 1 on?
            CC      CONV02          ;yes- call CONV02
            RRC                     ;is bit 2 on?
            CC      CONV03          ;yes- call CONV03
            RRC                     ;is bit 3 on?
            CC      CONV04          ;yes- call CONV04
            .
            .
            .
            RRC                     ;is bit 7 on?
            CC      CONV08          ;yes- call CONV08
            .                       ;program continues
            .

CONV01:     PUSH    PSW             ;must save accum and flags
            .                       ;program goes here
            .                       ; .
            .                       ; .
            POP     PSW             ;restore state
            RET                     ;return for next check
```

In this example the byte to be tested was first loaded into the accumulator. The byte was then rotated, followed by a conditional call. Since each subroutine being called preserves the accumulator, the routines can be stacked one after another to test each of the eight bits. A macro could be used in place of each rotate and conditional call statement, which would make the program more readable as follows:

```
TSTBIT   MACRO    ADDRESS      ;test the least
         RRC                   ;significant bit of
         CC       ADDRESS      ;the accum, if on call
         ENDM                  ;specified address

         LDA      BYTE         ;get byte to test
         TSTBIT   CONV01       ;call CONV01 if bit 0
         TSTBIT   CONV02       ;call CONV02 if bit 1
         •                     ; \ rest of routines
         •                     ; / go here
         TSTBIT   CONV08       ;call CONV08 if bit 7
         •                     ;rest of program follows
         •
```

8
Real-Time Executives

WHAT IS A REAL-TIME EXECUTIVE?

The previous chapters have discussed various design and programming techniques to aid you in your assembly-language programming. But there is also an entirely different technique for developing complicated assembly-language programs which involves the use of a real-time executive.

A real-time executive is a program that runs other programs. It is an operating system that runs in the background on your computer. This new program will be transparent to your applications program. It controls and allocates all the microprocessor resources and in effect gives your microprocessor a number of new instructions.

This chapter will discuss what real-time executives can do, how they operate, their limitations, and the special features available under them. Real-time executives can be a powerful tool for the assembly-language programmer.

Real-Time

A good question at this point is, what is meant by "real time"? It is difficult to understand the term "real-time executive," if the first two words don't make sense. A program that operates in real time is capable of keeping up with any input that it was designed to receive. (It does what you want in the expected amount of time.) The program on your microprocessor development system that allows you to type in characters is operating in real time. If, however, you became a speed typist, you might be able to outtype your computer. In this case the computer would no longer be operating in real time. Real-time programs can quickly become non-real-time, if their inputs occur faster than they can be handled.

The majority of microprocessor products operate in real time. These devices can range from blenders and microwave ovens to industrial robots. They must keep up with some set of physical inputs and produce some type of output, all within a specified period of time. This does not imply, however, that these programs must all operate quickly. In the case of a microprocessor-controlled tire balancer, the calculations needed to balance a tire might take four seconds to perform. In operation the machine spins a tire and then brakes the spinning tire to a halt. If the calculations can be performed before the tire stops spinning, the program can be said to be operating in real time even though the process takes four seconds. In this case the program operates in real time because there are no additional inputs to the system while it is busy calculating, and no one notices this fact.

Executives

You might also ask, what is a "real-time executive"? A real-time executive is simply a program that runs on your microcomputer system. This program acts as an operating system for the computer. An operating system can be found on all microprocessor development systems. When you type on the development system keyboard, a program or operating system receives and acts upon the characters you are typing. These keys are translated into commands and are then acted upon by the operating system. A real-time executive performs much the same function. Usually it is customized to your particular application or product.

The real-time executive allocates the microprocessor resources among the various program modules. Microprocessor resources are typically limited: there is only a fixed amount of memory space and computer time to do a given task. Real-time executives are programs that allocate these resources on a programmer-specified basis. Essentially, a real-time executive applies a fixed set of rules (made by the programmer) to the distribution of computer time and memory to the various program modules that make up the software system.

Real-Time Problems

Real-time programs written in assembly language have additional problems aside from those mentioned in Chapters 3 and 4 on top-down design and structured programming. These additional problems are related to the speed requirements of your program. Keeping up with one or two input lines and performing some function based on these inputs is not very difficult. Problems arise when the number of inputs and outputs grows. Monitoring 15 different inputs and performing 15 different output functions can become quite complex.

A real-time executive is designed to help you overcome these difficulties associated with writing real-time software. It can allocate or distribute sections of EPROM and RAM memory to various program modules. It can also allocate the microprocessor processing time to various program modules. Additionally, it may allocate some of the hardware resources found in your product. Not only does it allocate the various microprocessor resources, it also simplifies the real-time program itself. By taking over some of the specialized hardware and software-control functions of your system, the real-time executive makes your programs easier to design, manage, and maintain. Your programs will also become shorter in length, since you use code residing in the real-time executive.

EXECUTIVE CONCEPTS

There are five basic programming concepts involved in real-time executives: program tasks, concurrency, priority, suspension, and reentrant code. None of these concepts is normally used in assembly-language programming, but under a real-time executive each becomes very important.

Program Tasks

A program task is a short, self-contained piece of software typically dealing with only one logical function. It must execute in a short amount of time. In programming under a real-time executive, there are also certain other restrictions placed on program tasks. Tasks may not wait for input functions to change or for time to go by. This implies that all short program loops that wait for something to occur should be avoided. All these functions have been taken over by the real-time executive, which performs them much more efficiently.

Since program tasks do not wait for inputs to occur or for time to go by, they execute in much less time than they normally would.

This gives the microprocessor system more time to perform its functions. A program task typically has a structure that is similar to that of a subroutine. Under a number of real-time executives a program task ends with a return instruction. This command returns control to the real-time executive.

```
;******************************************************
;* THIS TASK CHECKS SIX STATUS PASSED IN THE C REG.  *
;* IF ANY BITS WERE SET IT WILL SET A FLAG TRUE. IT  *
;* THEN RETURNS TO THE REAL-TIME EXECUTIVE.          *
;******************************************************

TASK1:    MOV    A,C          ;get the status word
          ANI    0FCH         ;check for bits 7–2
          JZ     TSKEXT       ;if 0- quit
          MVI    A,TRUE       ;otherwise set flag
          STA    TFLAG        ;to true
TSKEXT:   RET                 ;common exit point
```

Concurrency

Under a real-time executive the various program modules that make up a system can be considered to be running concurrently. Programs that run concurrently look as if they are all running at the same time. Of course, the microprocessor can only execute one instruction at a time; the real-time executive cannot change that basic fact. However, the executive can rapidly enable one program and disable another. This rapid interchange of program tasks makes it appear as if all programs are running concurrently.

Concurrency can be a very useful feature. Suppose you have 25 input lines that may all change at random. Every time a line goes from a zero to a one, you must toggle a corresponding output line for one second. You must also keep track of a keyboard, display, and printer. This kind of program can be a nightmare to write in assembly language. With concurrent programming you simply write 25 separate routines, each one handling a single input bit. The real-time executive will switch these tasks on and off, and for all practical purposes it will look as if these 25 separate tasks are running concurrently. The other portions of the program are handled in the usual way.

Priority

When a programmer designs a system, some portions of that system are more important than others. Under a real-time executive some tasks are more important than others or should be performed in a specified order. A real-time executive gives the programmer the ability to assign fixed or variable priorities to each program task. This ensures that tasks with a high priority will be run ahead of others with lower priorities. The concept of priorities gives the programmer the ability to make one task run before another. It can also be used to keep one task from interrupting another by assigning them different priorities. This feature can be used to avoid writing reentrant program modules.

Suspension

Once program tasks have priority, program scheduling problems can arise. Suppose a very low-priority program is running. If an interrupt occurs that schedules a high-priority task to be run, this task will be ignored until the lower priority task is finished. Some mechanism must be supplied by the real-time executive to stop the low-priority task and allow the high-priority one to be run in its place. Task suspension performs this function. It allows any program to be suspended (put to sleep) by a higher priority program which is then run in its place. When the higher priority program is finished, the suspended program will be started up where it left off.

While the task-suspension function supplies a useful feature, it also places certain restrictions on the programmer. Every task can be suspended by a higher priority one. It is up to the programmer to see that each task he writes is transparent to suspension. Any routine you write may be suspended in the middle of its operation. Your routines must tolerate this when running under a real-time executive. This is another reason why tasks may not wait in loops for time or inputs to change. The task could be suspended while in the middle of the loop, causing it to miss its time count or lose an input signal.

Reentrant Code

The task-suspension feature of a real-time executive can cause some interesting problems in programming. Consider a program task that it currently running. If that task is suspended by a higher priority program which then calls or runs the first program task again, what will happen? The result will depend upon how the first task was written. If this task was written as a reentrant module, everything will work correctly. But if the program is not reentrant, a serious error will occur. Furthermore, that error will be extremely hard to debug, since it will occur only at random intervals when the first task is interrupted by the second.

A reentrant program is one that may be interrupted anywhere in its operation and rerun again without affecting the first pass or run through the program. Reentrant programs have a problem in using RAM variables. If a program has a fixed RAM area or variables that it uses, then it cannot be reentrant. The first pass through the routine would set the RAM one way. When the program was interrupted, the second pass through it would begin. The second pass would change the RAM contents. When the interrupt ended, the first pass through this routine would be lost since its RAM has been changed. The easiest way to make a task reentrant is to keep all information the module needs in the microprocessor's internal registers. If the routine is interrupted, this information will be saved, ensuring that the program will function correctly.

Real-time executives often offer memory management techniques that enable you to write reentrant tasks using RAM. They do this by allocating sections of RAM to programs upon request. Once allocated, this memory belongs to the program that requested it and cannot be used by another program or the same program running reentrantly. This feature of a real-time executive will be discussed in more detail in a later section of this chapter.

REAL-TIME EXECUTIVE FEATURES

Real-time executives typically offer a number of built-in features that are of great help in writing real-time programs. They could be

Events

DEVENT   Number
(Declare Event) Declare that event 'Number' has occured. All tasks waiting for this event will be run as soon as their priority allows.

WEVENT   Number 1, Number 2, . . . Number N
(Wait for Event) Suspend this task until event 'Number1' or 'Number2' or . . . 'NumberN' has occured. Program execution will commence at the instruction following this macro command.

Task Scheduling

SCHED   Task,Priority
(Schedule) Tell the executive to run Task as soon as it's Priority will allow. Task is the address of the beginning of the program module.

Time

TIMESC   Task,Priority,Time
(Time Schedule) Instruct the executive to run Task after the amount of Time specified has expired. Task will be run after this time based on the Priority assigned.

WTIME   Time
(Wait Time) Suspend this program until Time has expired. Program execution will commence at the next instruction following this macro command.

Memory Management

ADDBUF   Anchor,Buffer
(Add Buffer) Add the Buffer specified to the queue specified by Anchor.

GETBUF
(Get a Buffer) Get a buffer from the executive. Pointer to this buffer will be returned in the HL register pair.

POPBUF   Anchor
(Pop a Buffer) Remove the first (top) buffer from the queue specified by Anchor. A pointer to this buffer will be returned in the HL register pair.

RELBUF   Buffer
(Release a Buffer) Give the specified Buffer back to the executive so it can be reused.

REMBUF   Anchor,Buffer
(Remove a Buffer) Remove the specified Buffer from the queue indicated by Anchor. Buffer will be removed from anywhere in queue.

Where:

Anchor = Collection of pointers to a queue

Buffer = Address of assigned memory area, typically fixed length

Number = Event number to wait for or declare (1–32)

Priority = Task priority level (0–7)

Task   = Name, (address) of task to run

Time   = Amount of time to wait in milliseconds

Figure 8-1. Commands supplied with a real-time executive. These are a set of commands supplied with a hypothetical real-time executive. The commands are actually macros and are supplied in a library file.

duplicated with application software but would be difficult to design, write, and implement. These special features include various means of time and measurement and control, software events, memory management, and system calls. Figure 8-1 shows a list of commands supplied with a typical real-time executive. These commands are supplied in a macro library.

Scheduling Tasks

Any executive must give you some way of starting program tasks. There is typically an unconditional method of starting a task. You use a macro command to pass the task starting address (its name) and a priority to the executive. This command informs the real-time executive that the task exists and should be run according to the passed priority. From this point on the executive will control the execution of this task.

```
        •                       ;program proceeds
        •                       ;normally
        STA     MFLAG           ;set a flag
        SCHED   MOTOR,5         ;schedule MOTOR to run
        MVI     C,3             ;at priority 5, then
        •                       ;proceed normally
        •                       ;with rest of program

MOTOR:  LDA     MFLAG           ;task is small
        •                       ;program
        •                       ;that ends
        •                       ;with a
        RET                     ;return
```

Time Control

One of the commonest features of a real-time executive is the ability to control tasks based on time. The executive will run a program task after some fixed amount of time has passed. The programmer can vary the time from milliseconds to minutes. Thus one program task may schedule a different program, or itself, to run in a fixed number of seconds. The executive uses the time between these two tasks to run other programs.

```
;******************************************************
;* THIS ROUTINE DEBOUNCES FIVE INPUT PORTS.  IT      *
;* LOOKS AT THE PORTS ONCE EVERY 50 MS AND SAVES     *
;* THEIR VALUES IN RAM.  OTHER ROUTINES ONLY         *
;* EXAMINE THE RAM IMAGES WHICH ARE DEBOUNCED.       *
;******************************************************


           DSEG


INP01:     DS        1              ;RAM image of port 1
INP02:     DS        1              ;through 5 saved here
INP03:     DS        1
INP04:     DS        1
INP05:     DS        1


           CSEG


SCAN:      IN        PORT01         ;\ read a port
           STA       INP01          ;/ and save in RAM
           IN        PORT02         ;\ repeat for
           STA       INP02          ;/ each parallel port
             .
             .
             .
           IN        PORT05         ;\ read last port
           STA       INP05          ;/ and save
           TIMESC    SCAN,2,50      ;schedule this program to
           RET                      ;run in 50 ms. priority 2
```

Another form of time control is task suspension for a fixed period. A program task can have the ability to suspend itself for a fixed period of time, after which the task will be restarted exactly where it left off. This gives your programs the ability to turn themselves off for a period of time.

```
;******************************************************
;* ONCE STARTED, THIS PROGRAM WILL FLASH A LIGHT     *
;* ONCE EVERY TWO SECONDS.  CLEARING BUSYFG WILL     *
;* STOP THE FLASHING.                                *
;******************************************************
```

```
FLASH:   STORE    BUSYFG,TRUE     ;enable this routine
FLSH10:  LOAD     BUSYFG          ;check to see if
         RZ                       ;still allowed to run
         MVI      A,1             ;running- then
         OUT      PORTA3          ;turn on light
         WTIME    1000            ;wait 1000 ms (1 sec)
         MVI      A,0             ;\ now turn
         OUT      PORTA3          ;/ off light
         WTIME    1000            ;wait 1000 ms
         JMP      FLSH10          ;go run it again
```

These forms of time control allow you to write programs that can do almost any time-related function with ease. Switch debouncing is simple to do. A routine can schedule itself to run every 40 milliseconds and save the value of a switch state in RAM. Since contact bounce on a switch is usually limited to 10 to 20 milliseconds in length, this effectively debounces the switch. Any other routine that needs to read the debounced switch has only to look at the RAM image of this switch. Causing an output line to go on and off for two seconds is also easily accomplished. All these timing functions leave the microprocessor free to do other tasks while a routine is waiting for some amount of time to pass.

Software Events

A second feature of many real-time executives involves software declared events. A software event is a method by which one program or task can communicate with another. There are usually two different commands associated with this feature: one allows a task to declare that an event has occurred, while the other allows a task to suspend itself until a particular event or group of events occurs. Use of software declared events can simplify the way in which your programs are designed and written. One program module can wait for a switch input to happen, while a second module reruns itself every 50 milliseconds to look for this switch input. When the switch input occurs, the second module simply declares that the event has happened, and this starts the task that was waiting for the switch running. This allows you to separate the switch detection function from the part of the program that acts on this information.

```
;***************************************************
;*  THIS MODULE DETECTS A PARTICULAR BIT GOING FROM  *
;*  A 0 TO A 1.  WHEN THIS OCCURS AN EVENT IS DECLARED  *
;***************************************************

SWITCH   EQU       1                    ;give a label to the event

         DSEG

OLD:     DS        1                    ;previous switch status

         CSEG

PHYSIN:  IN        PORT80               ;physical input module
         ANI       4                    ;read port and get bit
         MOV       C,A                  ;save for exit
         JZ        PHYBYE               ;if not there- exit
         LDA       OLD                  ;otherwise compare
         XRA       C                    ;to last time, look
         JZ        PHYBYE               ;for 0 − 1 transition
         DEVENT    SWITCH               ;declare it occurred
PHYBYE:  MOV       A,C                  ;common exit- save
         STA       OLD                  ;new as old
         TIMESC    PHYSIN,3,50          ;schedule this again in
         RET                            ;50 ms. at priority 3
```

```
;***************************************************
;*  THIS MODULE WAITS FOR A PARTICULAR EVENT AND ACTS  *
;*  ONLY AFTER THIS EVENT HAS OCCURRED.              *
;***************************************************

WAITSW:  WEVENT    SWITCH               ;suspend task until event
         MVI       A,1                  ;event has occurred so
         OUT       PORT81               ;turn on bit
         WTIME     1000                 ;for 1 second (1000 ms)
         MVI       A,0                  ;now turn off
         OUT       PORT81               ;bit, and
         JMP       WAITSW               ;then go wait again
```

Memory Management

Another function of a real-time executive is memory management. In a previc section, reentrant coding problems were discussed.

Software modules that use RAM have a problem being made reentrant. If your real-time executive has memory-management features, almost any task can be made reentrant. These memory-management features can also be used to pass information between program modules.

Real-time executives perform memory-management functions by working from a pool of memory that is permanently assigned to the executive. Any task that needs RAM may ask the executive for some memory. The executive will then allocate a fixed amount of its RAM to that program. That piece of RAM now belongs to the task that requested it, until such time as it releases this memory back to the executive. No other task will have access to this memory until it is released to the executive. If a program keeps asking the executive for pieces of memory and never gives any of this memory back, the real-time executive will eventually crash.

A task can be made reentrant by using this memory-allocation feature. The task must ask the executive for a piece of RAM at its start. As long as it uses only this RAM and the microprocessor registers, it will be reentrant. If the routine is interrupted and run again before its completion, the new version of it will ask for a new section of RAM from the executive. Since each run of the task uses different pieces of RAM, they will not interfere with one another. When the task finishes, it must release the RAM section back to the executive.

Real-time executives can also supply other memory-management features beyond the simple allocation of RAM. Memory is often allocated in fixed length units called buffers. Real-time executives can supply several useful routines that work with these buffers. One type of routine allows the programmer to chain or link together a number of buffers. These buffers then form a linked list or queue, as discussed in Chapter 7. Other routines allow a programmer to remove the first item or any other item from a queue. By using these buffers and queues, the programmer can develop sophisticated means for passing information from module to module.

```
;*****************************************************************
;* PASS INFORMATION FROM INTERRUPT 7 TO A ROUTINE TO    *
;* HANDLE THAT DATA IN A FIFO MANNER.                   *
;*****************************************************************
```

```
            DSEG

TRNANC: DS          4              ;anchor for a data queue
POINTR: DS          2              ;pointer to data


            CSEG

INTINI:    GETBUF                  ;initialize by getting
           SHLD       POINTR       ;a buffer and saving the
           RET                     ;pointer away

INTER7:    LHLD       POINTR       ;interrupt routine gets
           IN         DATA         ;pointer and data item
           MOV        M,A          ;put character in buffer
           INX        H            ;move pointer
           SHLD       POINTR       ;and save
           CPI        CR           ;this end of message?
           JNE        INT7EX       ;no- jump
           ADDBUF     TRNANC       ;yes- put this buffer on
           GETBUF                  ;queue and get a new
           SHLD       POINTR       ;buffer for interrupt
INT7EX:    end the interrupt
           .
           .
           RET                     ;end of interrupt
```

```
;*******************************************************
;* ANALYZER ROUTINE FOR DATA.  PROCESSES DATA IN  *
;* A FIRST IN FIRST OUT MANNER.                    *
;*******************************************************

ANALYZ: POPBUF     TRNANC       ;get the top buffer from
        .                       ;the queue
        .                       ;process this data
        .                       ;and when done
        RELBUF                  ;release the buffer back to
        RET                     ;the executive
```

System Calls

A final feature of a real-time executive involves system calls. These calls are specialized entry points into the real-time executive. They allow the programmer to use some of the internal features of the executive for his own purposes. System calls typically come in a macro library. They give the programmer English-like commands that utilize all the various features of the executive. There will be macro commands for time control, software events, memory management, and interrupt control. By using these macros, the programmer can avoid having to know anything about the internal organization and operation of his real-time executive. He simply uses the macro commands supplied with the executive.

DRAWBACKS OF REAL-TIME EXECUTIVES

With all these excellent features, real-time executives seem too good to be true. What costs and drawbacks are involved in using one? Do these operating systems cause more problems than they help solve? What problems will they make worse, and what new problems will they introduce?

Overhead

A real-time executive runs on your microcomputer. Since it is a program, it must take some amount of time to run. The amount of time the microprocessor spends executing real-time executive code instead of your program code is called overhead. It would be nice if there were no executive overhead. But since there is, how much time will the executive use?

The amount of time consumed by the executive is not that easy to measure, because it depends on the tasks you write that run under it. For example, you could have a real-time executive with no program tasks running under it, in which case the executive uses 100% of the microprocessor's computing time. As you add more and more tasks for the executive to control, the time consumed by the executive will decrease until it reaches some minimum − typically, 10% to 25% of the available computing time.

While that amount of time may seem excessive, it really is not. Because of the way you must write programs for real-time executives, you actually gain more time that the executive uses. Most microprocessor programs spend a good deal of time in program loops waiting for an input bit to change, or for some amount of time to go by. The real-time executive eliminates the need for these types of program loops, so you gain all this time back. A typical microprocessor program converted to run under an executive will actually have more spare computing time left than it did before the conversion.

Memory Requirements

Real-time executives require some EPROM and RAM space – another drawback to their use. Some limited microprocessor systems will not be able to use an executive, simply because of these memory requirements. However, most microprocessor systems don't have to worry about this. Usually, programs written under an executive need less code than the corresponding program written without an executive. This program savings makes up for the amount of EPROM space the executive consumes.

Executives vary greatly in length. Some minimal executives for eight-bit microprocessors occupy only 256 bytes of EPROM. A more typical size is in the range of 1.5K to 3K. Real-time executives also require some RAM space. This space is usually dependent upon the nature and number of tasks that you have running under the executive. The executive itself will need some private RAM, as well as a fixed RAM area from which it can construct buffers. For medium-sized assembly-language programs (10K to 25K), a RAM space of 1K to 2K is needed.

Price

A real-time executive can be purchased from an outside vendor or you can write the executive yourself, but either choice has its cost. A purchased executive can be quite expensive and may have software support problems, while writing and debugging your own executive can be difficult.

The are versions of real-time executives available for nearly every major microprocessor. The pricing of these executives varies, depending upon whether the user wants object or source code. Fees for object code run from $2,000 to $3,000, while source code is much more expensive, ranging from $5,000 to $20,000. In some cases source code is not available at any price. In addition to these charges, there may also be a license fee running from $50 to $100 per system sold. But lower fees can often be negotiated, depending upon the quantity of systems you sell.

Writing your own executive has an inherent cost. It will take time to design, code, and debug an executive. Because of the complexity of the executive, it may be difficult to totally debug it in a limited amount of time. If you are on a tight schedule, you can end up releasing a microprocessor product with bugs in its real-time executive. To estimate the cost of writing your own executive, you must consider not only the amount of time it will take to produce this software, but also the cost involved in a possible fault in your released product or system.

Debugging under a Real-Time Executive

A major drawback to a real-time executive is that debugging a program under it can be difficult. While an executive can be used to simplify your software, it can also complicate it if you are not careful. An executive gives you the ability to separate cause from effect in your software. One program module can scan for input changes, while another waits for those changes to occur. This logical separation can cause debugging problems at first. A data-flow diagram of your system can help you trace through your program from cause to effect (see Chapter 3).

Once a programmer has some experience with a real-time executive, debugging will become easier. Programs written under an executive tend to operate in a chained manner. One program module might look for an input. When this input occurs the first program module activates a second module and passes it the information. The second module processes the information and passes it to a third module that will handle these results. This type of program debugging may be different from the kind you are used to and can therefore be difficult at first. If you remember to create and use a data-flow diagram, you should have no problem following your program logic.

Another debugging difficulty has to do with program module interactions. Unless a real-time program is carefully designed, one program module may interfere with another under rare conditions. This type of error is nearly impossible to duplicate, since it happens at random, so that debugging it is very difficult. This type of problem can be avoided by using a good top-down design for your program and by implementing that design through structured programming techniques.

PROGRAMMING UNDER AN EXECUTIVE

Programming under a real-time executive is quite different from normal assembly-language programming. As you have seen in the previous examples, the executive offers many special features that are difficult to implement in a normal program. These features are powerful enough to change the basic way you design your programs.

Programs written for real-time executives tend to function in series. One program detects an event, then activates a second program that collects the data associated with this event and passes it on to a third module. This module then produces a result that is sent on to an output routine. All these routines are essentially chained together by the executive. The programs can be written in this fashion because the real-time executive makes the programs appear to be running concurrently.

Real-time executives can offer a number of special functions: sophisticated time control of programs, software declared events, and memory management (see Figure 8-1 on p. 000). Each of these functions can be of great use in your programming. They can eliminate much of the code you would have to write in order to perform each of these basic functions.

The easiest way to understand the advantages that come from programming with a real-time executive is to look through the previous programming examples in this chapter. Various features that are typically hard to implement in a normal assembly-language program are easy to do under a real-time executive. These sophisticated features are of most use when performing complicated tasks requiring concurrent programming and assembly language.

9
High-Level Languages

WHAT IS A HIGH-LEVEL LANGUAGE?

Just about every programmer knows how to use at least one high-level language. Unfortunately, it is often difficult to implement an entire microprocessor program in such language. But it would be useful to combine programs written in assembly language with those written in a high-level language. This chapter will answer some basic questions about high-level languages: what are they, and how can they be used with assembly language?

In assembly language there is a one-to-one correspondence between the assembly-language statements you write and the object code generated by the assembler. Each assembly-language statement you write generates one machine instruction. But in a high-level language this is not the case. One statement in a high-level language can generate numerous machine instructions. Generally, the higher the level of a programming language, the more machine instructions generated per statement.

It is easier to program in a high-level language than in assembly language. The high-level language has more powerful statements, is less concerned with program details, and is easier to write programs with. Usually it is also easier to document, test, and maintain a high-level language program than one written in assembler. Figure 9-1 shows the relationship between various high-level languages and assembly language. The further to the right you go on this chart, the higher the level of the programming language. From this chart it is possible to get some feel for the relationships among various programming languages.

All the advantages of high-level languages stem from the fact that these languages are closer to English than assembly language. The ultimate high-level language would be the English language itself. If English could be used as a programming language, stating the problem would be equivalent to coding the program. Unfortunately, since no

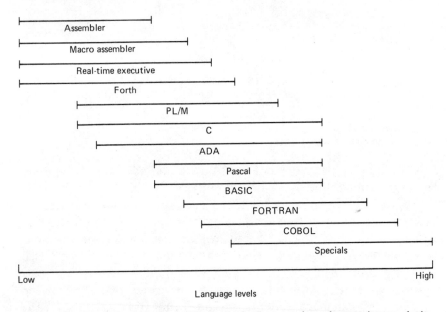

Figure 9-1. Language relationships. The level of a language depends upon its complexity. Assemblers are the lowest level language. Special-purpose languages can generate tremendous amounts of code with a single statement.

computers as yet understand English, you must at best use a high-level language to solve your programming problems.

One frequently stated reason for using high-level languages is that, being close to English, they are self-documenting. Nothing could be further from the truth. Even if programs could be written in English, they would still need comments and documentation. The best a program can do is tell you how something is being done. The program needs comments and documentation to tell you what is being done and the reasons behind the operation. Thus high-level languages do not remove the requirement for comments and documentation.

USING ASSEMBLY AND HIGH-LEVEL LANGUAGES TOGETHER

Separate the Logical from the Physical

Ideally, all programming should be done in a high-level language. Programmers are more efficient and produce better code in a high-level language. Unfortunately, for reasons that will be discussed, assembly language is often exclusively used to write microprocessor programs.

High-level languages can eliminate a number of the problems found in assembly-language programs. Even a well-documented, structured assembly-language program can be difficult to understand. High-level languages also offer a number of logical functions not easily implemented in assembly language. It is much more difficult to make logical errors in high-level languages than in assembly language.

In working with microprocessors, there are a number of reasons why assembly language is still preferred. A good assembly-language programmer can generate programs that are considerably more efficient than any produced by a high-level language. This is important, if the microprocessor's resources are very limited. Efficiency may relate to either program-execution speed or memory requirements. Often this efficiency is required by the microprocessor system. Some types of hardware or interrupts may be utilized only with assembly language. Thus there are reasons for using assembly language in your programming. However, this does not mean that you must write your entire program in assembly language.

One program technique that works well on microprocessors is mixing high-level language programs with assembly language. This is done by separating programs into portions that logically seem to fit into either assembly or a higher level language. The basic technique for doing this is to separate the logical or decision-making portion of your program from the physical or hardware-dependent portion.

When working in assembly language, it is normally a good idea to separate the logical section of a program from its physical side. This ensures that changes in the hardware or physical characteristics of your system do not affect the logical or decision-making portion. This breakpoint is also a good place to separate a program into high-level and assembly-language sections. All the logical or decision-making portions of your program can usually be implemented in a higher level language. The physical or control portion of your program typically works best in assembly language. Once your program is divided up in this manner, you can always go through the high-level sections and selectively recode those portions that need the speed of assembly language.

To separate programs in this manner, it is necessary to have some way of interfacing assembly language to a higher level language. There are a large number of high-level languages available for microprocessors, and a majority of them offer some method for interfacing to assembly language. By choosing a good high-level language that easily interfaces to assembly language, you can take the logical portion of your program and encode it entirely in that high-level language. Similarly the physical portion of your program can reside in assembly language. All that is required to do this is a good means of communicating between the two halves of your program.

Interfacing Assembler and High-Level Languages

There are various methods for communicating between high-level and assembly-language program modules. The method used will vary, depending on the high-level language used. There are five different ways in which high-level languages can pass information to assembly language.

Using Registers.   One method for passing information back and forth uses the microprocessor registers and stack. The actual means by which information is passed back and forth depends upon which high-level language is chosen and the microprocessor used. Specific languages will have slightly different ways of passing information back and forth. Normally, information is first passed in the microprocessor's registers. When the high-level program calls an assembly-language module, the microprocessor registers will contain the data that must be passed to the assembly-language routine. If the assembly-language routine needs more information than the registers can hold, the stack is typically used to contain the excess data. Information is passed back to the high-level language in exactly the same manner. These techniques work only with high-level languages that have specific support for them. This type of high-level language will typically generate relocatable object modules after a compile.

```
;********************************************************
;* THIS ROUTINE IS CALLED BY A HIGH-LEVEL LANGUAGE     *
;* IT MUST SEARCH THROUGH MEMORY FOR A 0FFH. IT IS     *
;* PASSED THE STARTING MEMORY ADDRESS IN REGISTERS     *
;* BC, AND A COUNT IN DE. IT MUST RETURN A TRUE OR     *
;* FALSE FLAG IN DE DEPENDING ON WHETHER THE 0FFH      *
;* WAS FOUND AND THE POINTER TO THE CHARACTER IN BC.   *
;********************************************************
```

```
SEARCH:   MOV    H,B          ;\ put pointer to
          MOV    L,C          ;/ memory in HL
SRCH10:   MOV    A,M          ;get a character
          CPI    0FFH         ;is it 0FFH?
          JNZ    SRCH20       ;no- jump
          MVI    A,TRUE       ;yes, set found char
          JMP    SRCBYE       ;go to common exit
SRCH20:   INX    H            ;otherwise, move pointer
          DCX    D            ;decrement counter
          MOV    A,D          ;\ check to see
          ORA    E            ;/ if counter 0
          JNZ    SRCH10       ;no- repeat routine
          MVI    A,FALSE      ;yes- set bad flag

SRCBYE:   MOV    E,A          ;save status in DE
          MOV    D,A          ;finish off upper register half
          MOV    B,H          ;\ put pointer back
          MOV    C,L          ;/ into BC
          RET                 ;return to other module
```

Using Calls. Another technique for interfacing these two languages involves the use of fixed-location calls. Some high-level languages will not allow information to be passed in registers between modules. All they allow is the ability to call a "machine" language subroutine. This ability is not as limited as it sounds. By building up a jump table, you can add a number of assembly-language features to your high-level program. The following example shows this type of jump table.

```
          ORG    1000H

          MVI    A,0          ;jump table sets light
          JMP    LIGHT        ;number in A and jumps
          MVI    A,1          ;to LIGHT subroutine to
          JMP    LIGHT        ;turn it on
          MVI    A,2          ;100AH
          JMP    LIGHT
          MVI    A,3          ;100FH
          JMP    LIGHT
          MVI    A,4          ;1014H
          JMP    LIGHT
          MVI    A,5          ;1019H
          JMP    LIGHT
          MVI    A,6          ;101EH
          JMP    LIGHT
          MVI    A,7          ;1023H
          JMP    LIGHT
```

```
LIGHT:    CALL    XLATE       ;translate number to bit
          OUT     PORT75      ;turn that light on
          RET                 ;return to caller
```

In this example, a high-level program calls location 1000H to turn on light 1, location 1005H to turn on light 2, and so on. This gives the high-level program a number of assembly functions simply by calling slightly different addresses. This type of jump or vector table is very useful in performing *output* functions, but it is not of much use in doing input functions. Some other way must be found to pass information back and forth in a call-type situation.

Using Memory. Another way of passing information back and forth involves the ability to examine and modify memory contents. Some programming languages allow the programmer to examine and alter any memory location. When this is combined with the ability to call a "machine" language subroutine, almost anything can be done. Information can be put into fixed-memory locations, then the "machine" language subroutine is called. The subroutine gets all the information it needs from these fixed-memory locations. The results, if any, of this routine are then placed in other fixed-memory locations. Upon return, the high-level portion of the program has these results available at previously specified memory locations.

```
;***********************************************************
;*  SEARCH THROUGH MEMORY FOR A 0FFH CHARACTER.  *
;*  START AT ADDRESS FOUND IN POINTER AND GO FOR  *
;*  A MAXIMUM OF COUNT NUMBER OF TIME.  RETURN    *
;*  TRUE/FALSE VALUE IN STATUS, AND POINTER TO    *
;*  CHARACTER FOUND IN POINTER.                   *
;***********************************************************

          DSEG

POINTR:   DS    2             ;memory pointer passed here
COUNT:    DS    1             ;search count passed here
STATUS:   DS    1             ;search result returned

          CSEG
```

```
SEARCH:  LHLD    POINTR      ;get the pointer to memory
         LDA     COUNT       ; \ get counter
         MOV     C,A         ; / into C register ·
SRCH10:  MOV     A,M         ;get a character
         CPI     0FFH        ;is this an FFH?
         JNZ     SRCH20      ;no- jump
         MVI     A,TRUE      ;yes- set true
         JMP     SRCBYE      ;and exit
SRCH20:  INX     H           ;otherwise, move pointer
         DCR     C           ;decrement count
         JNZ     SRCH10      ;and repeat if necessary
         MVI     A,FALSE

SRCBYE:  STA     STATUS      ;put status here
         SHLD    POINTR      ;and pointer back
         RET                 ;return to caller
```

Using Object Modules. Some high-level languages, when compiled, generate relocatable object modules. These modules are often compatible with those produced by your relocatable assembler. This allows you to make up modules in each programming language and then link them together. Each language can reference variables and routines in the other. The linking locater resolves all these references automatically.

Using Primitives. One final technique for passing information back and forth between different languages involves the use of a primitive. A primitive is a short program that interfaces two other programs together. Primitives are used to enable high-level languages to use features of assembly-language routines such as real-time executives.

High-level languages can have a problem using all the features of a real-time executive. Usually the manner in which a high-level language can pass information to assembly language is not compatible with the way a real-time executive expects to receive its information. A primitive is a routine that translates information for these two routines. It rearranges or modifies the information that is to be sent to the real-time executive. But even if you do not have a real-time executive, you may need primitives. Your assembly-language program may have several subroutines that are used quite frequently. The manner in which information is passed to these subroutines may not be compatible with the manner in which your high-level language passes data to assembly language. In this case a primitive can be written that will translate this information into the proper form. Construction of a primitive is often preferable to rewriting all the assembly-language routines that call those particular subroutines.

REVIEW OF HIGH-LEVEL LANGUAGES

There are a large number of high-level languages already in existence. Most if not all of them have been implemented in some form or other on microprocessors. Choosing a high-level language for your microprocessor can be a difficult task. There are many languages available and no clear method for choosing one language over another. This review will examine what each high-level language is designed to do, how difficult it is to learn and use, and what it is like to program with it. The ability to combine assembly language with this high-level language will also be covered.

First, however, something should be said about program-language standards. Most high-level languages have a standard they are supposed to meet. This is a written specification usually developed by the American National Standards Institute (ANSI). Standardized languages include ADA, FORTRAN, COBOL, and Pascal. These standards are supposed to ensure that programs written in these languages are transportable from system to system and that language dialects are kept to a minimum.

When working with microprocessor systems, remember that almost no high-level language follows its standard exactly. Thus the language you learn on one microprocessor system is not quite the same as the one you must learn for another system. At best, it will be a different dialect; at worst, a different language. Any language that does follow its standard exactly will probably not be very useful to you, because high-level languages were usually invented for the minicomputer and mainframe environment and therefore do not take advantage of the microprocessor environment unless specifically adapted to it. (This is usually done by adding special commands like PEEK, POKE, IN, OUT, etc.) Compilers and interpreters written specifically for microprocessors rarely follow the standards set for them. This can cause problems in learning the language and making your programs portable from system to system.

Where does this leave us in our choice of a high-level language? There are lots of different languages, but no clear guide to choosing one. There are also standards, but they do not apply well to microprocessors. Standardization is so inadequate that often a program written in a particular high-level language will not run when transferred to the same language on the same micro, but developed by a different manufacturer. So you are better off with a language adapted to the microprocessor environment. That now leaves the choice of a high-level language. The best way to choose one is to take a look at a number of languages. Always remember that the original purpose of a language will greatly and permanently effect the way that language works and the type of problems it solves best.

Language Characteristics

A number of terms will be used to discuss the features and operation of various high-level languages. These terms help give a feel for what it is like to program in such languages.

A *compiler* is a program which generates machine code instructions from a high-level-language source file. The compiler translates the high-level statements into machine code that the microprocessor can understand. Once a program has been compiled, it is directly executable on the computer for which it was compiled.

An *interpreter* is a program that operates directly on a source file in memory. This program translates high-level language statements one at a time into executable routines. It then performs these routines immediately. Interpreters tend to be much slower than compilers.

A *modular* language allows programs to be designed, written, and tested as independent modules or tasks. Portions of a program may be written and compiled separately. They may be tested with or without the other modules associated with this program.

A *structured* language is one designed to support the structured programming techniques. It will usually support program statements like IF/THEN/ELSE and WHILE/DO. This type of language will probably not include a GOTO statement.

A *typed* language places restrictions on the definition and use of variables. Typically a variable must be defined as a certain type before it is used. The compiler will make sure that a variable of one type is not mixed with a variable of another type. Thus if you declare variable CHAR as a character type, only ASCII characters may be stored in it.

Ada

The Ada programming language has just recently been developed by the Department of Defense in cooperation with the United Kingdom, Germany, and France. The government would like to see one programming standard for all its software work. This fact alone makes learning to use this language a good idea. The Ada programming language is of recent design and therefore takes into account the best software engineering work done in the last few years. This language gives slightly more weight to business than to scientific problems. Another point to consider is that Ada was designed by a committee − a fact that has a significant effect upon its structure and features. Ada is a compiled language, modular and strongly typed. It lends itself well to the structured programming techniques developed in the last decade. Designed to improve software reliability, portability, and maintainability, it is expected to be the dominant language of the 1980s and 1990s.

Ada has a very large instruction set. This makes it difficult to learn. Large portions of the instruction set are so complicated that it is doubtful the entire language will ever be implemented on most microprocessors. The majority of these complicated instructions are not required to solve most problems. The Department of Defense has steadfastly refused to authorize any subset of the Ada programming language. Since the entire language will not fit into most microprocessors, you might think this will cause a problem. Never fear; there are already several unauthorized subsets of the Ada programming language available for microprocessors! Thus the Department of Defense has struck another blow against standardization of programming languages.

BASIC

The BASIC (Beginner's All-purpose Symbolic Instruction Code programming language was originally designed to instruct students in programming, hence it was intended to be extremely simple to learn.

BASIC was originally an interpreted language, but at the present time there are both interpreted and compiled versions available. There is no real standard for the BASIC programming language – in this case, an advantage. The lack of standards has allowed numerous improvements to be made to the language over the years. These improvements have added structured programming features to the language and changed it into a compiled language. The best versions of BASIC approach Pascal, PL/M, and C in structured programming ability.

Most BASIC languages allow some mix of assembly language and BASIC. Typically they allow calling machine language subroutines, examining memory, and changing memory (CALL, PEEK, and POKE). More advanced BASICs may also pass information concerning BASIC variables to the assembly-language program.

C

The C programming language is a general-purpose, relatively low-level language. It deals with the same objects that assembly language does, but with the all advantages that a high-level language can offer. The C language was developed to write compilers and operating systems. It is hard to discuss the C programming language without discussing its function library. The basic C language provides only minimal functions. There is no provision for input-output facilities. All these extra features are provided by libraries that are included with the compiler. This gives C an advantage when working with microprocessors. The basic language does not vary from one microprocessor to another; only its library functions change. This can also be a disadvantage, since the method for input and output can vary with each new operating system or microprocessor.

C is a compiled language that is modular, typed, and well structured. It is medium in difficulty to learn. Its syntax can be hard to read. C allows an easy mix of assembly language and itself. This is, in fact, how many of the library functions for it are created. Typically C programs may be compiled and then linked with assembly-language programs. The only real standard for C is *The C Programming Language* by Kernighan and Ritchie. The C language is an excellent replacement for assembly language.

Programming in C is quite different from working in other languages, owing to the features and structures available in it. Take the statement

```
++count;
```

This shows the use of the ++ operator, which means increment by one. This statement says: increment count by one. Note that there is no need for an equals sign. C has another interesting operator, the *. The * operator instructs the processor to fetch whatever the following item points at.

```
x = *pointer;
```

In this case x is assigned the value of whatever the pointer is pointing to. These two operators can be combined together:

```
x = *pointer++;
```

This statement says: let x equal whatever the pointer is pointing to and then increment the pointer by one. Note the differences between this form of programming and any other high-level language you are familiar with.

COBOL

COBOL (Common Business-Oriented Language) is a fairly old business-oriented programming language. It was designed to solve complicated business programming problems on mainframes and minicomputers. It is a compiled language, medium in difficulty to learn. It is not modular or structured. Because of its age, COBOL does not implement a number of the more modern structured programming techniques. While COBOL is available for a number of microprocessors, most business programs are now written in BASIC. Because of its age and business orientation, COBOL is not recommended for most microprocessor work.

FORTH

FORTH is an interesting new programming language with several serious drawbacks. It is a stack-oriented, dictionary-based programming language that utilizes reverse Polish notation. In FORTH, programs are broken down into a collection of very small subtasks. Each subtask is then defined as a part of the FORTH dictionary of functions. A task is then defined in the dictionary as a collection of subtasks previously defined. This process is repeated until the entire program is covered in a single dictionary definition. In this process the programmer is modifying the language definition until his program is a part of the FORTH language. Thus the language is truly extensible.

FORTH is an interpreted or compiled language that allows the programmer to mix assembly language with it. The major drawback to FORTH is the use of reverse Polish notation throughout. While reverse Polish notation works well on some calculators and is not too difficult to learn, it has serious drawbacks as a high-level programming language. The major problem is its lack of readability. The interpreted version can be quite slow, depending upon how many levels of dictionary nesting are used.

FORTRAN

FORTRAN (FORmula TRANslator) is one of the oldest high-level programming languages. Designed to solve scientific problems, it has now been adapted to commercial problems. Medium in difficulty to learn, FORTRAN is a compiled language that, depending on the version, may allow assembly language to be mixed with it. Because of its age FORTRAN is not a modular, typed, or structured programming language. Recent versions of it have attempted to implement some of these more modern features, but there will always be problems in modifying the basic structure of an old programming language. The best modifications can never make the language as good as one developed more recently. FORTRAN does a good job of solving complicated scientific problems on a large-scale computer. Though available for microprocessors, it is infrequently used. C, Pascal, and PL/M are all better choices for modern microprocessor languages.

LISP

LISP (LISt Processing) is a language that is oriented toward manipulating symbols and recursive data. Designed to solve problems in artificial intelligence, LISP is one of the oldest high-level programming languages. It is a continually evolving language with no formal standard. It is an interpreted language, and most microprocessor versions run quite slowly. It is medium in difficulty to learn. Assembly language is not allowed to be mixed with LISP. It is a modular, typed, and structured language. LISP statements can be very difficult to understand.

This language is list-oriented. It is designed to handle and process lists of information in much the same way that other languages use numbers and calculate or process data. LISP programs are capable of modifying themselves and thus "learning."

Pascal

Pascal is a fairly recent programming language. It was designed to teach students how to program and do systems programming. It is relatively easy to learn and is a compiled language. Most of the microprocessor versions of Pascal offer major exceptions to the standard. Thus some versions of Pascal allow you to mix assembly language with it, while others do not. Pascal is a strongly typed language and highly structured.

Programs written in Pascal consist of two major parts, the heading and the block. The heading identifies the program name and its parameters. The block consists of six separate sections: the first five contain label, constant, type, variable, and procedure declarations, while the last one contains the program statements. All programs written in Pascal must follow this structure.

PL/M

PL/M is one of the numerous subsets of the PL/1 programming language. Each microprocessor manufacturer seems to have a subset with a slightly different name. For this section all the different subsets can be considered similar, if not identical, to PL/M. The PL/M language was designed to solve programming problems. A highly structured programming language, it is medium in difficulty to learn. It is a compiled language. Most microprocessor versions of PL/M allow assembly language to be easily mixed with it. PL/M is modular, typed, and structured. The PL/M subset was designed to replace assembly language.

PREPROCESSING WITH HIGH-LEVEL LANGUAGES

Another use for high-level languages is becoming more and more popular — preprocessing. Preprocessors are translation routines used in conjunction with another language. Typically a preprocessor will take in an English-like file and translate this file into some form of assembly language. An assembler will then assemble this file and produce object code. The preprocessor operates as a special-purpose translator. It operates in much the same way that macros do in your assembler.

Why Use a Preprocessor?

Of what possible use is a preprocessor? It is generally used to translate the work of noncomputer programmers into a programming language, usually assembly language. This lets a nonprogrammer write or modify computer programs. Preprocessors are also often used to construct tables. These tables will be entered by someone who knows nothing about programming. The table entry will be in a form that is close to English. The preprocessor will translate this table into its composite assembly-language statements.

There are also other reasons for using preprocessors. Quite often they are used simply to reduce the complexity of a set of tables. They may also be used to give a programmer more complicated macros than are available under his assembler. Most uses of preprocessors involve some combination of the three reasons just mentioned.

When would you use a preprocessor? It is not too difficult to construct tables so complicated that they can not be written with macros. When tables get this complex, it is a bad idea to try to implement them in straight assembly language. You will make the person who enters these tables do a considerable amount of work. He is bound to make some mistakes, and the frequency of mistakes will rise with the complexity of the tables. If macros won't give you the features you need, then a preprocessor might be the answer. A preprocessor lets you encode your tables in a form that is close to English.

What Is a Preprocessor?

A preprocessor is a program, and it must be written for the specific application for which it is intended. Such programs are usually not very difficult to write, if written in a high-level language. You use the features of the high-level language to take care of programming details such as file access and other basic I/O. The actual logic of the program is usually not too complicated, being mainly concerned with translating one language into another.

Macros.   A preprocessor can be used to implement macro features for assemblers that do not offer them. Since preprocessors are functioning as translators, they in effect do much the same thing as a macro. If your assembler does not offer macros, a preprocessor can be written or purchased to add the macro feature to your programs. You write your programs as if you had a macro assembler, then run the preprocessor on your program file to translate the macros into assembly language. Finally, you assemble your program in the normal fashion.

Special Macro Features.   Preprocessors that offer macros can go beyond the normal macro features found in most assemblers. Often it would be useful to allow one macro to reference material generated by another macro. This feature is not supported by normal macro assemblers. A preprocessor, however, can be written that will give you this feature. This will allow you to construct complicated tables, using macros that reference other tables or other macros.

Tables.   Another use for preprocessors involves placing table information into a clearer format. The closer a table approaches English, the easier it will be to encode, understand, and debug. Macros are used to make table structures more closely resemble English. But sometimes macros do not come close enough to English to be useful, in which case a preprocessor can be used to permit tables to be entered in a true English-language format. The preprocessor translates the English-like tables into assembly language, taking some of the programming burden off the programmer.

Using a Preprocessor.   A typical use for a preprocessor often involves all three reasons previously mentioned. Suppose you are constructing a microprocessor-controlled vehicle that must find its way around a warehouse. The microprocessor must have some type of map in order to find its way around the building. A table structure must be developed to solve this problem. The question now arises, who defines the map for the microprocessor? The programmer who wrote the application program knows assembly-language programming very well, but probably knows little about material handling and warehouse operation. The person who designed the warehouse understands its operation completely, but knows nothing about programming.

It would be useful if the person who did the warehouse design could also do the tables for the microprocessor. The only feasible way to effect this is to use a preprocessor. This will allow the warehouse specialist to make an English-like table that defines his application. The preprocessor will then translate this into assembly language, whereupon the program can be assembled and the vehicle completed. The warehouse specialist has thus been given the ability to program the vehicle without learning assembly language.

From this example you can get some idea of what preprocessors can do. They are useful for reducing complicated table structures into a more readable English-like form. Preprocessors can also provide macro capabilities for assemblers that do not offer this feature, and give you more advanced or more complicated macros than are possible with your macro assembler. Preprocessors help bring your programs closer to English.

Appendix A
ASCII Character Set

LSD \ MSD		0 000	1 001	2 010	3 011	4 100	5 101	6 110	7 111
0	0000	NUL	^P	SP	0	@	P		p
1	0001	^A	^Q	!	1	A	Q	a	q
2	0010	^B	^R	"	2	B	R	b	r
3	0011	^C	^S	#	3	C	S	c	s
4	0100	^D	^T	$	4	D	T	d	t
5	0101	^E	^U	%	5	E	U	e	u
6	0110	^F	^V	&	6	F	V	f	v
7	0111	^G	^W	'	7	G	W	g	w
8	1000	^H	^X	(	8	H	X	h	x
9	1001	TAB	^Y	)	9	I	Y	i	y
A	1010	LF	^Z	*	:	J	Z	j	z
B	1011	^K	ESC	+	;	K	[	k	{
C	1100	FF	^\	,	<	L	\	l	|
D	1101	CR	^]	-	=	M	]	m	}
E	1110	^N	RS	.	>	N	^	n	~
F	1111	^O	US	/	?	O	—	o	DEL

Figure A-1. ASCII character set.

Appendix B
Working with Disks and Listings

Filing floppy disks

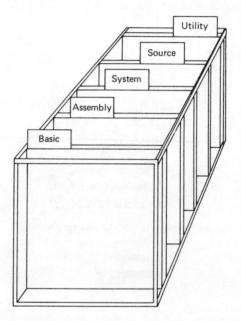

Figure B-1. Filing floppy disks. One method of filing floppy disks uses a standard hanging-file folder. This allows disks to be labeled by category and to be easily located.

Organizing disk backups

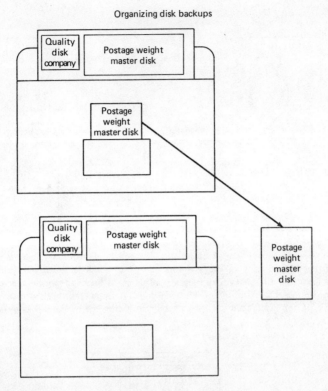

Figure B-2. Organizing disk backups. Remembering when to back up a disk can be difficult. One technique works as shown above. Each disk has an index card associated with it.
Any time a disk is worked on, the index card is removed from the disk envelope. Every few
days the index cards are collected and those disks are then backed up. Once a disk is backed
up, its index card is returned to the disk envelope.

Backing up a disk

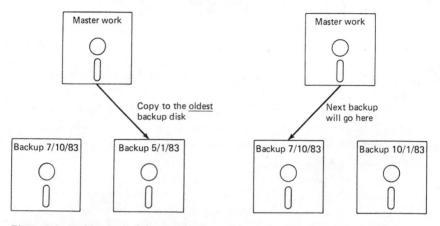

Figure B-3. Backing up a disk. Backing up a disk can be dangerous. There is always the possibility that both disks involved in the backup process will be destroyed. Thus it is important to have two different backup disks at all times. A backup from the master disk will be made to the older backup disk. This gives you a fairly current backup disk, in the rare event that both the master and the new backup are destroyed by the disk-copying process.

Modular listings

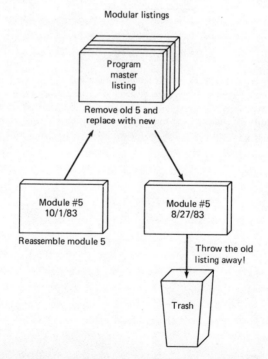

Figure B-4. Modular listings. Modular programs generate modular listings. When an individual module is reassembled, the new listing must replace the old one in the program master listing. This keeps the master listing up to date.

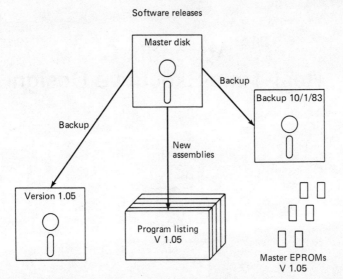

Figure B-5. Software releases. Software released to customers should have a good deal of documentation to support it. This documentation should include a complete listing of that software along with a labeled disk. Both items should be labeled with a version number. There should also be a master disk and two backup copies of it. All work is done on the master disk, not the last version disk.

Appendix C
Real-Time Executive Design

Schedule a task

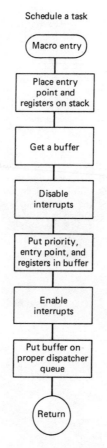

Figure C-1. Schedule a task.

Schedule a task to run after time has expired

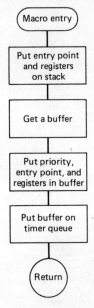

Figure C-2. Schedule a task to run after time has expired.

Suspend the current task for a fixed time

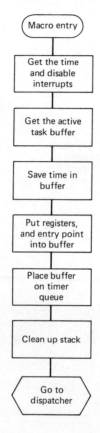

Figure C-3. Suspend the current task for a fixed time.

Declare event

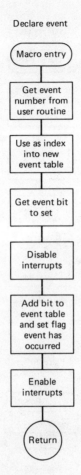

Figure C-4. Declare an event.

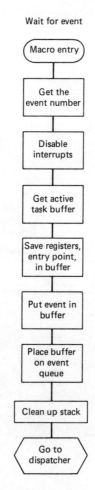

Figure C-5. Wait for an event.

Add a buffer to the queue

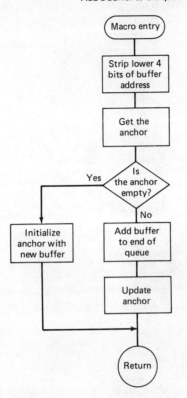

Figure C-6. Add a buffer to a queue.

Get a buffer from the buffer pool

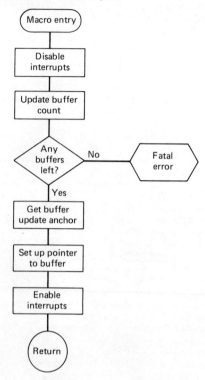

Figure C-7. Get a buffer from the buffer pool.

Pop a buffer from the top of a queue

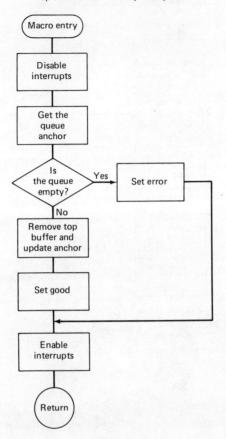

Figure C-8. Pop a buffer from the top of a queue.

Release a buffer back to the buffer pool

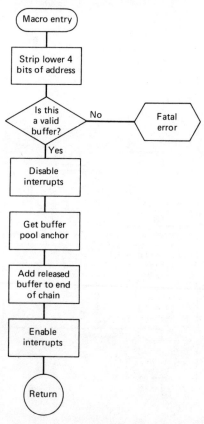

Figure C-9. Release a buffer back to the buffer pool.

Remove the specified buffer from the queue

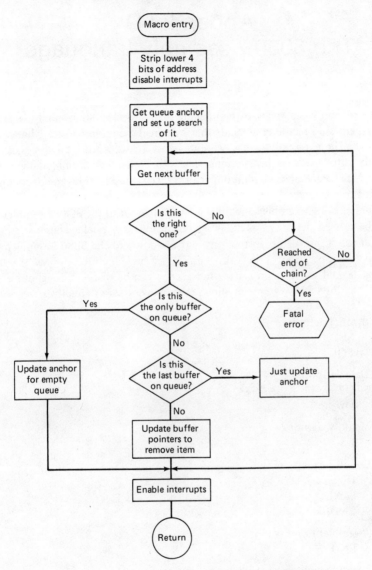

Figure C-10. Remove the specified buffer from the queue.

Appendix D
The 8080 Assembly Language

There are two basic types of commands in the Intel 8080 assembly language. First, there are specific commands that inform the microprocessor what it is to do next. These assembly-language statements are converted by the assembler directly into machine instructions. The other class of assembler commands instructs the assembler program to perform specific tasks. This type of command is called an assembler directive.

The following assembler directives are used to control the 8080 assembler and may be seen in the program examples throughout this book. These commands are not actual processor instructions, but directives to the 8080 assembler that modify the operation of that program. Assembler directives follow the same general format as program instructions. They can be placed throughout a program. The Intel 8080 assembler allows the following set of directives:

- Symbol definition
  SET
  EQU

- Data definition
  DB
  DW

- Memory definition
  DS

- Conditional assembly
  IF
  ELSE
  ENDIF

- Assembler termination
  END

- Location counter control
  ORG
  ASEG
  CSEG
  DESG

- Program linkage
     PUBLIC
     EXTRN
     NAME
     STKLN

ASSEMBLER DIRECTIVES

SET Directive

Label	Opcode	Operand
name	SET	expression

SET assigns the value calculated by "expression" to the name specified by the label field. The value of the specified variable may be changed by another SET command.

EQU Directive

Label	Opcode	Operand
name	EQU	expression

EQU assigns the value calculated in "expression" to the name specified in the label field. The value of the specified variable may not be redefined by any other command.

DB Directive

Label	Opcode	Operand
optional:	DB	expression(s) or string(s)

The DB directive instructs the assembler to store the data specified by "expression" or "string" in consecutive memory bytes, starting with the current location counter.

DW Directive

Label	Opcode	Operand
optional:	DW	expression(s)

The DW directive instructs the assembler to store the data specified by "expression" as 16 bit values in consecutive memory locations, starting with the current location counter.

DS Directive

Label	Opcode	Operand
optional:	DS	expression(s)

The DS directive instructs the assembler to reserve "expression" number of data bytes for future data storage. This command only reserves storage, it does not assemble any data into your program. It is used to reserve RAM storage space.

IF, ELSE, and ENDIF Directives

Label	Opcode	Operand
optional:	IF	expression
optional:	ELSE	—
optional:	ENDIF	—

These directives are used together to perform conditional assembly. Based on the evaluation of an expression, the assembler can be instructed to assemble different pieces of assembly-language code. The assembler evaluates the expression; if the result is TRUE, all code between the IF and the next ELSE or ENDIF statement is assembled. If the expression is FALSE, all this code is ignored. The ELSE directive is optional. If, when it is used, the expression evaluates to FALSE, then all statements between the ELSE and the next ENDIF are assembled.

END Directive

Label	Opcode	Operand
optional:	END	expression

The END directive tells the assembler to terminate each pass of assembly here. The optional expression will be evaluated, if present. This value will be used as a starting address for the program module.

ORG Directive

Label	Opcode	Operand
optional:	ORG	expression

The ORG directive sets the assembler location counter to the value specified by "expression."

ASEG Directive

Label	Opcode	Operand
optional:	ASEG	

The ASEG directive instructs the assembler to use the location counter to assemble code that is not relocatable. The ORG directive can be used to set or change the location counter.

CSEG Directive

Label	Opcode	Operand
optional:	CSEG	

The CSEG directive instructs the assembler to assemble all the following instructions in a relocatable format by using the code segment location counter.

DSEG Directive

Label	Opcode	Operand
optional:	DSEG	

The DSEG directive instructs the assembler to assemble all the following instructions in a relocatable format by using the data segment location counter.

PUBLIC Directive

Label	Opcode	Operand
optional:	PUBLIC	name-list

The PUBLIC directive instructs the assembler to make the symbols listed in "name-list" available for access by other programs.

EXTRN Directive

Label	Opcode	Operand
optional:	EXTRN	name-list

The EXTRN directive gives the assembler a list of symbols that are referenced in this program module but not defined here. They are defined in another program module and must be declared PUBLIC there.

NAME Directive

Label	Opcode	Operand
optional:	NAME	module-name

The NAME directive gives a name to the object module generated by this assembly. Module names are used for linking modules together into a program and for debugging that program.

STKLN Directive

Label	Opcode	Operand
optional:	STKLN	expression

The STKLN directive informs the assembler that "expression" number of bytes should be saved for the stack for this module.

INSTRUCTION SET

The following list defines the 8080 assembly-language instruction set. Certain abbreviations will be used for standard register names, addresses, and values as follows:

aa	=	16-bit address
n	=	number from 0 to 7
p	=	8-bit port address
r	=	an 8080 register name: A, B, C, D, E, H, L, M
rg	=	double-register stack pair: PSW, B, D, H
rr	=	an 8080 double-register name: B, D, H, SP
v	=	8-bit value
vv	=	16-bit value

ACI	v	Add immediately the value v with carry to the accumulator.
ADC	r	Add r to the accumulator with carry, where r is the contents of any single register or the memory location pointed to by HL.
ADD	r	Add r to the accumulator, where r is the contents of any single register, or the memory location pointed to by HL.
ADI	v	Add immediately the value v to the accumulator.
ANA	r	AND the contents of register r (or the memory location pointed to by HL) against the accumulator.
ANI	v	AND immediately the value v against the accumulator.
CALL	aa	Call the subroutine aa.
CZ	aa	Conditional subroutine; call if zero flag set.
CNZ	aa	Conditional subroutine; call if zero flag not set.
CP	aa	Conditional subroutine; call if accumulator positive.
CM	aa	Conditional subroutine; call if accumulator negative.
CC	aa	Conditional subroutine; call if carry set.
CNC	aa	Conditional subroutine; call if carry not set.
CPE	aa	Conditional subroutine; call if parity flag even.
CPO	aa	Conditional subroutine; call if parity flag odd.

CMA		Complement the accumulator.
CMC		Complement the carry.
CMP	r	Compare the accumulator with the register contents r, or the value of memory pointed to by HL.
CPI	v	Compare the accumulator with the value of v.
DAA		Decimal adjust the accumulator into 2 BCD digits.
DAD	rr	Add the contents of register pair rr, or the stack pointer, to register pair HL.
DCR	r	Decrement register r or the memory location pointed to by HL.
DCX	rr	Decrement the register pair rr or the stack pointer.
DI		Disable interrupts.
EI		Enable interrupts.
HLT		Halt the processor.
IN	p	Input byte from port p to accumulator.
INR	r	Increment register r or the memory location pointed to by HL.
INX	rr	Increment the register pair rr or the stack pointer.
JMP	aa	Jump to the address aa.
JZ	aa	Conditional jump to address aa, if zero flag set.
JNZ	aa	Conditional jump to address aa, if zero flag not set.
JP	aa	Conditional jump to address aa, if accumulator positive.
JM	aa	Conditional jump to address aa, if accumulator negative.
JC	aa	Conditional jump to address aa, if carry set.
JNC	aa	Conditional jump to address aa, if carry not set.
JPE	aa	Conditional jump to address aa, if parity flag even.
JPO	aa	Conditional jump to address aa, if parity flag odd.
LDA	aa	Load the byte specified by address aa into the accumulator.
LDAX	rr	Load the accumulator, using the double-register pointer rr (only D and B allowed).
LHLD	aa	Load the HL register pair with the 16-bit value that aa points to.
LXI	rr, vv	Load register pair rr with 16-bit value vv.
MOV	M, r	Move the contents of register r into the memory location pointed to by HL.

MOV	r1, r2	Move register r2's contents into the specified register r1.
MOV	r, M	Move the contents of the memory location pointed to by HL into register r.
MVI	r, v	Move immediately to register r, or memory location pointed to by HL, the value v.
NOP		No operation.
ORA	r	OR the accumulator against the contents, or the specified register or memory pointed to by HL.
ORI	v	OR the value v with the accumulator.
OUT	p	Send the contents of the accumulator out to port p.
PCHL		Jump to the address specified in HL.
POP	rg	Pop the specified register pair off the stack.
PUSH	rg	Push the specified register pair onto the stack.
RAL		Rotate carry and accumulator left.
RAR		Rotate carry and accumulator right.
RET		Return from subroutine.
RLC		Rotate accumulator left and into carry.
RRC		Rotate accumulator right and into carry.
RZ		Conditional return, if zero flag set.
RNZ		Conditional return, if zero flag clear.
RP		Conditional return, if accumulator positive.
RM		Conditional return, if accumulator negative.
RC		Conditional return, if carry set.
RNC		Conditional return, if carry not set.
RPE		Conditional return, if parity flag even.
RPO		Conditional return, if parity flag odd.
RST	n	Restart n, call subroutine at address n*8.
SBB	r	Subtract the register specified, or the memory location pointed to by HL, from the accumulator with carry.
SBI	v	Subtract the value v from the accumulator with carry.
SHLD	aa	Store the value of HL starting at location aa.
SPHL		Load the stack pointer from HL.
STA	aa	Store the accumulator at location aa.
STAX	rr	Store the accumulator where register pair rr points to (only B and D allowed).

STC		Set the carry.
SUB	r	Subtract register r, or the memory location pointed to by HL, from the accumulator.
SUI	v	Subtract the value v from the accumulator.
XCHG		Exchange the DE register pair with the HL pair.
XRA	r	Exclusive OR register contents r, or memory location pointed to by HL, with the accumulator.
XRI	v	Exclusive OR the value v with the accumulator.
XTHL		Exchange the top stack item with HL.

Appendix E
Microcomputer Buzz Words

Initial exposure to the world of microcomputers can be quite traumatic. It may seem as if there is an infinite amount of new information to learn, and to top this off, no one speaks English! (At least it doesn't *sound* like English.) But you can't join the club unless you know the jargon. The following section will explain what most of these buzz words mean.

BIT

As in "I will have a bit of pie." Actually, a bit of pie would not be very satisfying, since a bit is a unit of binary information. It may take a value of either 1 or 0.

BUG

Any of an order (Hemiptera-Heteroptera) of insects with forewings thickened toward the base and an affinity for wrecking software. Also, any problem is software.

BYTE

Try not to confuse this with a bite of that bit of pie you wanted before. Bytes and bits are related. One byte usually represents 8 bits. Numerically this can represent a number from 0 to 255.

DEBUG

Pest control, as applied to software testing.

DEVELOPMENT SYSTEM

A mythical yet expensive tool for software development that Hercules used to quickly and easily solve his 12 prodigious labors all before lunch. This collection of hardware and software is used to develop and debug software.

EEPROM

Electrically erasable programmable read-only memory. A device that was named solely so as to be confused with EPROM. It is an EPROM, only it can be erased by electricity instead of ultraviolet light.

EPROM

Electrically programmable read-only memory. A memory device which can be programmed by a special box and also erased so as to be reused at a later date. To be erased, the device must be exposed to ultraviolet light. These devices must all have little clear windows on their tops. Hope this doesn't disillusion those of you who thought the windows were there to let you admire some IC specialist's work.

EXECUTIVE   Probably not one of the people that works with Daddy at the office. More likely, a piece of software that is in charge of the rest of the programs at the office.

FIFO   Refers to a first-in, first-out buffer. Something like the ideal toaster: you could keep putting more bread in it, while perfect toast keeps coming out the other end. The first piece of bread you put in will be the first piece of toast that comes out.

FLOPPY
DISKS   A good place for putting things like your programs. They come in several sizes but are not too easy to accidentally swap. Basically, a medium-speed mass-storage media.

IN-CIRCUIT
EMULATOR   A mystical device used to communicate with other hardware. It will let your development system hardware talk to your product hardware, unless they come from different families.

INFINITE   Much bigger than a bread box. The number of hours of software work needed to complete the current project correctly.

I/O DEVICES   Input/output devices! Do I have to tell you everything?

MACRO   A fancy way of typing less but saying more.

MICROSECOND   One millionth of a second. Yes, that's 1/1,000,000. Most microprocessors take a few microseconds to complete an instruction cycle.

MILLISECOND   One thousandth of a second. Considering that human reaction time is measured in hundreds of milliseconds, this is still pretty fast.

MODEM   A device used by juvenile delinquents to harass other juvenile delinquents who happen to own big computer systems. It allows computer systems to talk to each other by sending information in the form of tones over phone lines.

NANONEWTON   An incredibly technical-sounding piece of jargon that has no meaning whatsoever. Use it to impress your friends.

NANOSECOND   One billionth of a second. About the amount of time it takes light to travel 11.8 inches. Digital circuitry operates in the nanosecond range. Frightening, isn't it?

PRINTER BUFFER	An incredibly stupid device that serves a useful purpose. It adjusts the flow of information from your (fast) computer to the flow of information that your (depressingly slow) printer can handle.
PROGRAM COUNTER	Usually referred to as the PC, unless you own an IBM PC, which would make that usage more confusing than this explanation. The program counter is a pointer in the microprocessor that tells it where the next instruction is to come from.
RAM	An acronym for random access memory — memory that can be read from or written to. Think of it as a friend (RAF) who not only talks to you but also listens.
REAL TIME	The ability to complete a task within the time allotted to it.
ROM	An acronym for read-only memory. This is similar to those friends of yours who only talk, never listen.
RS-232	An old standard for sending serial information that everyone talks about but no one ever seems to follow completely. When someone talks about RS-232 signals, he probably means the EIA standard RS-232 25 pin connector. What signals he intends to use in that connector is anyone's guess.
SERIAL	An interesting and economical way of getting information from here to there. The information is sent in series. It's cheap on wiring but really needs a piece of hardware (UART) to decode and send the signal.
STACK	Much the same as a stack of pancakes. In this case, however, you are more interested in stacking data. The microprocessor contains a pointer to memory. This memory functions as a first-in, last-out buffer. When you call a subroutine, the return address is pushed onto the stack. To return, you pop it off the stack.
TERMINAL	A device used to communicate with a computer, typically featuring a display and keyboard. Don't confuse the name of the device with how you feel after entering data into it for 10 hours. Besides, it could have been worse: power could have failed five minutes before you finished!

UART   Universal asynchronous receiver transmitter. Also to be confused with USRT and USART. Never mind the differences — they all send and receive serial data in one way or another. They are all hardware devices that simplify your software by sending and decoding information serially.

WORD   When your boss calls you to his desk to have a word with you, he will definitely not have 16-bit numbers on his mind. For most microprocessors, a word is two bytes or 16 bits.

Index